The Presley Family & Friends Cookbook

The Presley Family & Friends Cookbook

A Cookbook and Memory Book
from Those Who Knew Elvis Best

Donna Presley Early, Edie Hand,
Darcy Bonfils, Ken Beck, and Jim Clark

CUMBERLAND HOUSE
Nashville, Tennessee

PUBLISHED BY
CUMBERLAND HOUSE PUBLISHING, INC.
431 Harding Industrial Drive
Nashville, Tennessee 37211-3160

Cover design by Harriette Bateman.
Text design by Julie Pitkin.

Library of Congress Cataloging-in-Publication Data

The Presley family & friends cookbook : a cookbook and memory book from those who knew
  Elvis best / Donna Presley Early . . . [et al.].
      p.   cm.
  Includes index.
  ISBN 1-888952-75-X (paperback)
  1. Cookery, American—Southern style. 2. Presley, Elvis, 1935–1997. I. Early,
  Donna Presley, 1950– .
TX715.2.S68P74   1998
641.5975—dc21   98–21681

3 4 5 6 7 8 — 08 07 06 05 04 03

Contents

Acknowledgments

*W*e wish to thank all of the Presley family members, friends, fans, and restaurants that shared favorite recipes, photographs, and memories for this book. (Attributions of recipe contributors accompany the recipes themselves.)

We're also most grateful to all of the people who generously helped us gather material from all over the world for this book. We wish to thank Christy Rogers, Marian Cocke, Mary Jenkins, Karen Sue Pritchett, Betty Hofer, Ed. Cassidy, Carlene Sowards, Marsha Kinsaul, Gerry Mitchell, Carol Butler, Roxie Kelley, April Heeren and United Media Syndicate, and artist Guy Gilchrist.

We also appreciate the contributions to this book from all of the staff at Cumberland House, including publisher Ron Pitkin, editor Julie Pitkin, Lori McNeese, and publicist Mary Beth Trask. Thanks also to cover designer Harriette Bateman.

Donna would especially like to thank her dear grandmother Minnie Mae Presley and her beloved mother, Nash Presley Pritchett, for giving her recipes for living, as well as for some good cooking.

Edie wishes to express her love and appreciation to some of the great cooks in her life, including her mother, Sue Hacker Hardesty, and her grandmother Alice Hood Hacker. She also thanks her sister, Kim Blackburn Poss, for her love and support and Ben Speer for his support, efforts, and encouragement.

Darcy thanks her mother, Marjorie Bonfils, whose home cooking and recipes helped shape who she is. She also thanks Marvin Schechter for his counsel.

Ken thanks his wife, Wendy, daughter, Kylie, and son, Cole, for their patience and help. Jim thanks his wife, Mary.

This book has been a global team effort and we appreciate the efforts of all who helped make it possible!

Introduction

*T*his special blend of favorite recipes, cherished photographs, and wonderful memories from the Presley family, friends, and colleagues has been compiled with love and affection. It takes us back to some of our most favorite times!

As we were gathering recipes from close to home and around the world in tribute to Elvis and his music, warm feelings from earlier days came flowing back. For instance, Edie remembers standing beside her grandmother Alice (niece of Elvis's grandmother Minnie Mae Presley) in her kitchen as Edie, covered with flour, enjoyed learning how to bake homemade biscuits and chocolate gravy. (You'll find this family recipe inside.)

Besides the nourishment from great Southern cooking, we also received nourishment from one another. Donna remembers spending many happy hours through the years sitting around the dining room and kitchen tables at Graceland and at other family homes, where family members shared their private thoughts, their joys, and even their sorrows.

You'll find delicious recipes, rare photographs, and remembrances shared here by a broad range of Elvis's relatives, close friends, and fans—fine folks such as the Blackwoods, the Jordanaires, the Speer family, and others who created such powerful music with Elvis. Also kindly sharing recipes are people who worked with Elvis on the concert trail and elsewhere. And providing delicious recipes for some of the foods that Elvis himself enjoyed most is his longtime cook at Graceland, Mary Jenkins, who also shares her memories of Elvis.

We also felt it was especially important to include recipes from some of Elvis's admirers from around the world. Our cookbook honoring Elvis simply wouldn't be complete without including his fans, who are the people most responsible for keeping his music and memory alive, "forever and always."

Elvis enjoyed food as much as any other all-American Southern boy, and this cookbook features platter after platter of some of his favorite foods, straight from the kitchens of some of his most beloved cooks—taking you on a culinary tour from Graceland to "Blue Hawaii."

We hope you enjoy this Presley family scrapbook of recipes and photographs, cooked up by Elvis's family, special friends, and extended family of fans.

And we hope this cookbook takes you back to some favorite times with your own family and friends. Maybe it will even be a source for new favorite moments for you—both in the kitchen and at the dinner table.

The Presley
Family & Friends
Cookbook

Starters

★ SEE SEE C. C. RIDER SAUSAGE CHEESE DIP ★

1   **pound ground beef**
1   **pound pork sausage**
1   **teaspoon garlic powder**
2   **dried red chili peppers**
2   **pounds processed cheese, cubed**
1   **medium onion, minced or 1 table-**
    spoon dehydrated onion
1   **12-ounce can prepared jalapeño**
    and tomato salsa mix
1   **10¾-ounce can mushroom soup**
1   **medium red pepper, chopped or**
    crushed

In a large frying pan cook the beef and sausage with the garlic powder and chili peppers until the meat is done. Pour off the fat from the pan.

In the top of a double boiler over simmering water melt the cubed cheese over medium heat. Add the onion, jalapeño and salsa mix, mushroom soup, and red pepper. Add the meat mixture to the cheese and mix all well. Keep it on the stove until the mixture is hot.

Serve with tortilla chips for a real south of the border taste! May be served hot or cold.

Serves 10.

Georgann Reynolds
Elvis Country Fan Club

★ EASY CHEESY CHEESE DIP ★

1   **pound Roquefort cheese, room tem-**
    perature
2   **8-ounce packages cream cheese**
1   **medium onion, grated**
    Parsley, chopped
    Steak seasoning sauce, to taste

In a large mixing bowl mix the cheeses together. Add the onion and season to taste with parsley and steak sauce. Chill.

This is an easy dish that is a real crowd-pleaser! Serve with chopped vegetables or chips.

Serves 10.

Edie Hand
Cousin of Elvis Presley

*As a teenager, Elvis snapped this photo of himself
in a dime store photo booth.*

★ C'MON EVERYBODY CRAB DIP ★

1   8-ounce package cream cheese,
      softened
½   to ¾ cup light mayonnaise
1   teaspoon creamy or regular horse-
      radish sauce
1   teaspoon dry or prepared mustard
1½ tablespoons minced onion
2   tablespoons chopped or dried
      parsley
    Dash garlic powder
1   8-ounce can crab meat, drained

In a large bowl blend together the cream cheese, light mayonnaise, horseradish sauce, mustard, and onion. Fold in the parsley, garlic powder, and crab meat and mix well.

Serve with sliced, raw vegetables, or crackers.

If pressed for time, make this in advance and keep it chilled in the refrigerator until needed. This also tastes great heated!

Serves 6 to 8.

Rose-Ann Bernett
Canadian National Elvis Tribute Fan Club

★ DIDJA' EVER DILL DIP ★

2   cups sour cream
1½ cups mayonnaise
1   tablespoon dill weed
2   tablespoons minced onion
2   teaspoons seasoned salt
    Fresh vegetables

In a large mixing bowl mix the sour cream, mayonnaise, dill weed, minced onion, and seasoned salt together until creamy. Refrigerate.

Chop up colorful, fresh vegetables and serve together.

Serves 6.

Verna Melohn
Elvis fan

★ SAND CASTLES SALMON BALLS ★

1   **15½-ounce can red salmon**
1   **egg**
1   **cup corn flakes, crumbled**
    Pinch salt
    Salad oil

In a medium mixing bowl place the salmon and remove the bones and skin. Crack the egg into the salmon and add the corn-flake crumbs and salt, mixing thoroughly. Roll into balls about the size of walnuts. Place on waxed paper.

In a saucepan heat 1½ inches of salad oil until very hot. Drop the balls into the hot oil and cook until golden. When done, remove the balls from the oil with a strainer and cool on a plate covered with a paper towel.

Makes about 15 to 20 balls.

Edie Hand
Cousin of Elvis Presley

The Films of Elvis Presley

Love Me Tender (1956)
Loving You (1957)
Jailhouse Rock (1957)
King Creole (1958)
G.I. Blues (1960)
Flaming Star (1960)
Wild in the Country (1961)
Blue Hawaii (1961)
Kid Galahad (1962)
Girls! Girls! Girls! (1962)
Follow That Dream (1962)
It Happened at the World's Fair (1963)
Fun in Acapulco (1963)
Roustabout (1964)
Viva Las Vegas (1964)
Kissin' Cousins (1964)
Tickle Me (1965)
Harum Scarum (1965)
Girl Happy (1965)

Paradise, Hawaiian Style (1966)
Frankie and Johnny (1966)
Spinout (1966)
Easy Come, Easy Go (1967)
Double Trouble (1967)
Clambake (1967)
Speedway (1968)
Live a Little, Love a Little (1968)
Stay Away, Joe (1968)
Charro! (1969)
The Trouble With Girls (1969)
Change of Habit (1969)

Plus:
Elvis: That's the Way It Is (1970)
Elvis on Tour (1972)

All of these films are on video and most are available from
Movies Unlimited at 1-800-4-MOVIES.

★ SONG OF THE SHRIMP DIP

1	**8-ounce can shrimp**
3	**tablespoons chili sauce**
2	**teaspoons lemon juice**
⅓	**cup mayonnaise**
1	**8-ounce package cream cheese, softened**
1	**rib celery, sliced**
1	**green pepper, sliced**
	Crackers or chips

In a large mixing bowl combine the shrimp, chili sauce, lemon juice, and mayonnaise and mix together well. Add the softened cream cheese and mix well with a blender or hand mixer.

Serve as a dip with sliced celery, green peppers, crackers, and chips.

Serves 8.

Shirley Beattie
Presley-ites Fan Club
Orlando, Florida

Even as a young man, Elvis loved to wear distinctive belts.

★ ALL THAT I AM ALASKAN SALMON FRITTERS ★

1	**7½-ounce can Alaskan salmon**
¼	**cup milk**
1	**egg, slightly beaten**
1	**teaspoon lemon juice**
1	**cup buttermilk baking mix**
½	**teaspoon seasoned salt**
¼	**cup finely chopped celery**
2	**tablespoons finely chopped green pepper**
2	**tablespoons finely chopped onion**
	Oil for frying

In a small bowl drain the salmon, reserving the liquid. Flake the salmon with a fork. In a separate bowl add the milk to ½ cup of the reserved liquid. Add the egg and lemon juice, and mix well. In a large bowl combine the buttermilk baking mix and seasoned salt. Add the liquid mixture, and blend in the salmon and vegetables, mixing well.

In a deep fryer heat the oil to 375°. Drop the batter by spoonfuls into the oil. Cook for about 3 minutes or until golden brown on both sides. Drain on paper towels. Serve with lemon wedges and seafood sauce or tartar sauce.

Serves 8.

Babe C. Crossman
Elvis Country Fan Club

Elvis presents a young fan with a ring and a scarf...

★ CROSS MY HEART SALMON CROQUETTES ★

1	16-ounce can salmon
1	medium onion, chopped
1½	cup crushed saltines
2	eggs, beaten
¼	cup self-rising flour
	Oil

In a mixing bowl place the salmon and remove the skin and bones. Mash the salmon to separate it slightly. Add the onion, saltines, eggs, and flour and stir until well blended. Form the mixture into balls in the palm of your hand, using about 2½ ounces of mixture for each ball.

In deep fryer or skillet heat the oil. Drop the balls into the hot oil and fry until brown. Drain in a colander or on paper towels.

Serves 8.

Betty Jo McMichael
Co-owner, Whistle Stop Cafe
Irondale, Alabama

...and a warm hug.

★ MEMORIES COCKTAIL MEATBALLS ★

1   **pound ground beef**
¼   **cup milk**
1   **teaspoon salt**
⅛   **teaspoon pepper**
1   **egg**
½   **cup dry breadcrumbs**
⅓   **cup minced onion**
1   **tablespoon parsley, snipped**
½   **teaspoon Worcestershire sauce**
¼   **cup shortening**
1   **10-ounce jar grape jelly**
1   **10-ounce bottle chili sauce**

In a large mixing bowl combine the ground beef, milk, salt and pepper, egg, breadcrumbs, onion, parsley, and Worcestershire sauce. Mix all together well and gently shape into 1-inch balls. Place the balls on waxed paper and set aside.

In a large skillet melt the shortening and brown the meatballs. Remove the meatballs and drain off as much fat as possible. Add the chili sauce and the jelly to the skillet, stirring constantly until the jelly is melted. Add the meatballs and stir until thoroughly coated. Simmer uncovered for 30 minutes.

Makes about 5 dozen.

Georgann Reynolds
In memory of Jackie Proescher
Elvis Country Fan Club

THE FIRST GUITAR THAT ELVIS EVER
STRUMMED WAS A GIFT FROM HIS MOTHER.
HIS UNCLE VESTER TAUGHT HIM A FEW BASIC
CHORDS, AND ELVIS'S OWN NATURAL SAVVY
AND TALENT TOOK OVER FROM THERE.

★ BY AND BY SAUSAGE BALLS ★

1   **pound hot sausage**
1½   **cups packaged biscuit mix**
2   **cups Cheddar cheese, grated**
    Cooking oil, if necessary

Preheat the oven to 350°. In a large mixing bowl mix the sausage, biscuit mix, and Cheddar cheese. Add oil if necessary to make it hold together. Roll into balls. Place the balls on a greased cookie sheet. Bake for 20 minutes.

Serves 6.

Verna Melohn
Elvis fan

Elvis looked sheik in this publicity photograph for 1965's Harum Scarum.

★ CHANGE OF HABIT CHICKEN WINGS ★

2	**pounds chicken wings**
1	**teaspoon salt**
½	**cup cornstarch**
1	**egg, beaten**
	Oil for frying
¾	**cup sugar**
	Pinch garlic salt or garlic powder
1½	**cups red wine vinegar**
1	**tablespoon soy sauce**
¼	**cup ketchup**

Rinse the chicken wings and pat dry. Separate at the joints. Place the wings, including the tips, in a saucepan and cover with water. Boil them until tender.

Drain the wings, discard the tips, and reserve ¼ cup of broth. In a nonstick skillet heat a small amount of oil. Sprinkle the wings with salt, and then roll in cornstarch. Dip the wings in the egg and place in the skillet. Fry until the wings are browned on both sides. Remove from the skillet and place in a baking pan.

Preheat the oven to 350°. In a saucepan combine the reserved broth, sugar, garlic salt, vinegar, soy sauce, and ketchup and mix well. Cook until the sugar dissolves, stirring frequently. Pour the mixture over chicken wings and bake for 30 minutes.

Serves 8 to 10.

Betty Jo McMichael
Co-owner, Whistle Stop Cafe
Irondale, Alabama

 ★ COCKTAIL CHEESE BISCUITS ★

½	**cup (1 stick) butter**
1	**cup shredded sharp Cheddar cheese**
1	**teaspoon salt**
¼	**teaspoon cayenne pepper**
1	**cup sifted all-purpose flour**
1	**8-ounce bag pecan halves**

Preheat the oven to 350°. In a large bowl cream the butter. Add the shredded Cheddar cheese and mix well. Add the salt, pepper, and flour to the mixture. Roll into small balls and place on a greased cookie sheet. Press a pecan half on each to flatten. Bake for 15 minutes.

Serves 10.

Deborah Long
Montgomery, Alabama

★ BAKED BRIE AND PASTRY ★

Brie, any size

1 **17-ounce package Pepperidge Farms flaky pastry sheets**

Preheat the oven to 375°. Wrap the brie snugly in the pastry sheets. Bake until the pastry is puffed and slightly brown.

Serve immediately on a platter with a cheese knife. Surround with crackers and fruit.

Harold Bradley

Elvis's cousins Edie Hand (left) and Donna Presley Early visit with renowned guitarist Harold Bradley at RCA's famed Studio B, where Elvis recorded many of his hits with Bradley.

★ KRISPY RICE CHEESE STRAWS ★

1   **cup (2 sticks) butter**
2   **cups grated sharp Cheddar cheese**
2   **cups all-purpose flour**
1   **teaspoon cayenne pepper**
2   **cups crispy rice puff cereal**

Preheat the oven to 375°. In a large bowl mix the butter and grated cheese together. Add the flour and pepper, and mix well. Blend in the cereal. Roll into small balls and place on an ungreased cookie sheet. Flatten with a fork. Bake for 10 minutes.
    Makes about a dozen.

Nonnie Kay Carnahan
Montgomery, Alabama

★ GRIDIRON CHOCOLATE MILK SHAKE ★

3   **scoops vanilla ice cream**
6   **ounces hot milk**
2   **ounces chocolate syrup**

Now, some might save this for dessert, but not Elvis. Goes great with the Palm Beach Burger.

Place the ice cream into a milk shake canister (or blender, if you don't have a shake machine). Add the milk and syrup. Mix in a milk shake machine until the ice cream is thoroughly mixed and smooth— no lumps.
    The folks at the Gridiron serve their shakes in the glass they use for iced tea. And they always give you the canister, too, so you don't miss one drop.
    Serves 1.

The Gridiron Restaurant
Memphis, Tennessee

★ FLIP-FLOP FRUIT SLUSH PUNCH ★

5   bananas, mashed

2   6-ounce cans orange juice frozen
    concentrate

2   10-ounce packages frozen strawber-
    ries

1   46-ounce can pineapple juice

    Juice of 5 lemons (or the equivalent
    of bottled lemon juice)

4   cups sugar dissolved in 6 cups
    water (heat briefly if necessary to
    fully dissolve)

4   quarts strawberry soda

In a pan or container with a lid combine all of the ingredients except the strawberry soda. Freeze (it will keep for 6 months).

Remove from the freezer 1 hour before needed. In a large bowl stir the mixture with a large spoon into slush while adding the strawberry soda.

Makes 6 quarts.

Betty Coker
Owner Lisa Marie *and* Hound Dog *airplanes,*
formerly owned by Elvis Presley
Memphis, Tennessee

Elvis's Leading Ladies (Part One)

Match the actress to the film.

1. Ursula Andress
2. Ina Balin
3. Joan Blackman
4. Donna Douglas
5. Shelley Fabares
6. Joan Freeman
7. Dolores Hart
8. Dodie Marshall
9. Mary Ann Mobley
10. Jocelyn Lane
11. Joan O'Brien
12. Cynthia Pepper
13. Nancy Sinatra
14. Judy Tyler

A. *Charro!*
B. *Clambake*
C. *Easy Come, Easy Go*
D. *Frankie and Johnny*
E. *Fun in Acapulco*
F. *Harum Scarum*
G. *It Happened at the World's Fair*
H. *Jailhouse Rock*
I. *Kid Galahad*
J. *Kissin' Cousins*
K. *Loving You*
L. *Roustabout*
M. *Speedway*
N. *Tickle Me*

ANSWERS: 1. E, 2. A, 3. I, 4. D, 5. B, 6. L, 7. K, 8. C, 9. F, 10. N, 11. G, 12. J, 13. M, 14. H

Nashville Songman Buddy Killen Remembers Elvis and "Heartbreak Hotel"

Alabaman-gone-Nashville Buddy Killen has been at the helm of hundreds of hit tunes. The former free-lance bass player for such singers as Jim Reeves, Hank Williams, George Morgan, and Ray Price became a song publisher with a young company named Tree in the mid-1950s.

By 1975 Killen had become president of Tree and by the time he sold the company to CBS in 1989, it was the top publisher of country music of all time. Not only did Killen serve as publisher of many of country music's greatest songs, but he also produced many of them as he worked in the studio with a myriad of vocalists, including Bill Anderson, T. G. Sheppard, Dinah Shore, Dolly Parton, Dottie West, and Ronnie McDowell, to name a few.

But it all starts with a song, and Tree's first huge hit was a little tune entitled "Heartbreak Hotel."

"The first time I met Elvis Presley was back-stage at the Grand Ole Opry. I saw this guy standing in a corner behind the stage, just shaking. He had his guitar slung over his back. I said, 'Hey, I'm Buddy Killen. What's the matter with you?'

"He said, 'I'm Elvis Presley and I'm scared to death. These people are going to hate me. If Sam (Phillips) would let me, I'd leave right now.'

"He calmed down a little bit, then he went on stage and did 'Blue Moon of Kentucky.' He shook 'em up pretty good. He still got a heck of a nice hand. That's the one time he appeared on the Grand Ole Opry."

Killen recalled that Presley cut at least five songs from the Tree Publishing catalog—songs such as "Green, Green Grass of Home," "Kentucky Rain," "Suspicious Minds," and "Always on My Mind," but it was "Heartbreak Hotel" that set the music world on fire back in 1956—not just for Elvis but for the fledgling company Killen had begun working for as well.

"Heartbreak Hotel" just exploded, Killen recalls. "I'd never seen anything like it. How'd I get involved with something that big? I was playing at the Mello Club in Daytona Beach.

"Mae Boren Axton always seemed to know where I was. She found me and I asked her, 'What are you doing here?' She lived in Jacksonville.

"She said, 'I'm here to see the Colonel (Tom Parker, who had a package show playing there, including Elvis, Hank Snow, and Andy Griffith). You want to go over with me?'

"'Sure,' I told her. So I went over to the audito-rium and stood backstage. I talked to Elvis, who just thought Hank Snow was the greatest thing since sliced bread. Elvis hadn't really taken off yet, but every city he played at, he left a star.

"Mae came back over to the Mello Club later, and she and I were sitting out there. I said, 'you've written some songs for other people. I'm working with a publishing company. Why don't you write something for me.'

"'I've got one song,' she said. 'I co-wrote it with Tommy Durden.'

"'What's the title?' I asked.

"'Heartbreak Hotel.'

"'Who do think it would be good for?'

"She said, 'Elvis. I'll send it to you.'

"When I got back home to Nashville I received a little five-minute reel-to-reel audio tape. Glen Reeves had done the demo with a guitar. He was singing the song like Elvis. So we got the song to Elvis, and he cut it. He was notorious for copying the demo. The performance you heard him do was Elvis singing like Glen Reeves singing like Elvis.

"He recorded the song in November, and at the end of February, 1956, they released it. It just became an overnight sensation. During that time the Colonel had made a deal to take over manage-ment of Elvis. They moved from Sam Phillips to RCA. Elvis recorded the song in Nashville at RCA Studios. Chet Atkins was actually the Nashville pro-ducer. It was the most amazing thing to watch. A career exploded just like that."

Buddy Killen owns The Stock-Yard in Nashville, ranked in the nation's Top 50 restaurants.

Buddy Killen in the studio.

★ BUDDY KILLEN'S FAVORITE MUSHROOMS ★

1   **8-ounce package mushrooms**
1   **teaspoon garlic salt**
1   **teaspoon pepper**
1   **teaspoon salt**
¼   **cup butter**

A few years ago, Carolyn and I used to spend a lot of time on our boat during the weekends, and I remember one time just sort of puttering around in the kitchen when I decided to fix a batch of mushrooms for our guests. Next thing I knew everyone there was raving about this simple little recipe. It seemed that our friends always enjoyed them so much I went ahead and put them on the appetizer menu at my restaurant.

Wash the mushrooms and let drain until as much water has been removed as possible. In a cast-iron skillet melt the butter and add the remaining ingredients. Cook over medium heat, stirring frequently, until the mushrooms are very brown.

*Buddy Killen, original publisher of "Heartbreak Hotel,"
and author of* By the Seat of My Pants:
My Life in Country Music *(Simon & Schuster)*

★ HEARTBREAK HOTEL HEARTY VEGETABLE SOUP ★

1	pound ground beef or turkey
1	46-ounce can V-8 juice
2	10¾-ounce cans cream of mushroom soup
1	20-ounce package frozen mixed vegetables
½	package cajun or favorite spice mix

In a large pot brown the meat. Drain. Add the other ingredients. Bring to a boil. Reduce the heat and simmer for 30 minutes. (To save time, the vegetables may be precooked in the microwave oven for 10 minutes.)

Makes 12 servings.

Claudia Gerlach
Lauterbach, Germany

Young newlyweds: Elvis's mother and father, Gladys and Vernon Presley.

★ BLUE SUEDE SHOES ★
CREAM OF BROCCOLI SOUP

8	cups water
3	broccoli stalks
1	small potato, finely diced
1	small carrot, diced
1	small onion, diced
1	rib celery, diced
2	cups milk
5	tablespoons margarine
7	tablespoons all-purpose flour
3	tablespoons chicken soup base

Pour the water into a large soup pot. Cut off the broccoli heads from the stalks. Cut the stalks down the middle and then into quarters. Place the stalks in the water and bring to a boil. Boil for about 15 minutes.

While the stalks are boiling, chop the broccoli heads and dice the rest of the vegetables. Remove the stalks from the water and add the milk and vegetables. Boil for about 10 to 15 minutes until cooked. In a small pan melt the margarine and blend in the flour. Pour the mixture into the soup and whisk until blended. Let thicken. Add the soup base. Let simmer.

Makes 5 to 6 servings.

Larry Wesley
Collingwood, Ontario
Canadian National Elvis Tribute Fan Club

★ KING CREOLE LOBSTER BISQUE ★

3	tablespoons butter or margarine
¼	cup chopped onion
3	tablespoons all-purpose flour
1	tablespoon fresh parsley
	Dash salt and pepper
2	cups milk
1	cup chicken broth
1¼	cups fresh or frozen lobster

In a large pot melt the butter and sauté the onion over low heat until tender. Stir in the flour, parsley, and salt and pepper. Cook until bubbly. Stir in the milk and chicken broth. Bring to a boil, but stir constantly. Stir in the lobster. Bring to a boil, then reduce the heat and cook for 3 minutes.

Makes 4 cups.

Carlene Sowards
Memphis, Tennessee

★ ELVIS'S FAVORITE HOMEMADE ★ VEGETABLE SOUP

2	**pounds stew meat**
1	**small onion**
1	**small green bell pepper**
1	**small clove garlic**
3	**15-ounce cans mixed vegetables**
5	**medium potatoes, cut up**
1	**15-ounce can okra**
	Salt and pepper to taste
3	**tablespoons sugar**

In a large pot cook the stew meat, onion, bell pepper, and garlic until the meat is almost brown. Add the mixed vegetables, potatoes, okra, and salt and pepper. Cook until the juice becomes thick. Add the sugar. Allow to simmer for about 2 hours and 30 minutes.

Serves 10.

Mary Jenkins
Personal cook for Elvis Presley

Meet Mary Jenkins: Graceland Cook for a Quarter of a Century

Mary Jenkins worked for Elvis Presley and his family at Graceland for more than twenty-five years, from 1963 until she retired in 1989 to take care of her ailing mother.

It all started because her late husband, who passed away in October 1997, was a taxicab driver. Mary happened to be riding with her husband one day while he was taking a Graceland employee to work.

"When she introduced herself, I asked did they need anybody else to work?" recalls Mary. "She said, 'No, but if they do, I will call and have them bring you out here.'"

The woman was true to her word, and sure enough, a while later Mary got a call to come to Graceland, where she was interviewed by Vernon Presley. "I talked to Elvis's daddy, and he hired me," she says, and it was as simple as that.

Mary began her long stay at Graceland as a maid. It was after Elvis married Priscilla that she applied her skills in the kitchen. "Priscilla called us

into the dining room and said, 'Daisy, you're no longer the cook. Mary, you're the cook, and Daisy, you're the maid,'" the cook recalls.

Mary got to know Elvis's tastes well. Elvis got to know and relish Mary's culinary talents even better. She says the king of rock 'n' roll had an all-American appetite that was partial to red meat and fresh veggies.

"He just ate regular home-cooked foods. He liked fresh vegetables for his dinner—creamed potatoes, crowder peas, string beans, mixed vegetables. And he loved hamburger steaks and roast beef. Sometimes he would have a ham steak, but he didn't like no poultry. Sometimes we could get him to eat a few little pieces of boneless chicken, but as for seafood, he did not like that," says Mary, who was born just south of the Tennessee state line in Hernando, Mississippi, and whose family moved the very next day to Memphis.

As for desserts, she says Elvis would flip over three special treats: banana pudding, lemon icebox pie, and caramel cake. "He was crazy about his banana pudding and lemon icebox pie," she says in her gentle, pleasant voice.

And what were Elvis's choices for beverages?

"He drank Pepsis, milk, and coffee. He would drink iced tea sometimes but was not crazy about it. Pepsis was the main thing."

As Graceland cook, Mary would wait in the kitchen during her shift. If Elvis or any family members wanted something to eat, they would call her on the phone from upstairs. Elvis might elect to have breakfast any time of the daylight hours.

"Just whenever he called," Mary says, she would cook his first meal of the day. "Sometimes he wouldn't call at all. He liked pork sausage and biscuits. He wanted his homemade biscuits. He loved bacon and eggs and oatmeal and grits for breakfast. We made his orange juice for him—squeezing the juice from fresh oranges."

Elvis obviously enjoyed Mary's meals, because he showered her with gifts, as he did many of his family, friends, and employees. "He bought this house for me," said Mary. "He bought me seven cars. He was good to me."

Both her house and one of the seven automobiles were gifts to Mary on Christmas Day of 1974. She remembers the day fondly. "He came with me to look at the house. He said, 'Mary, if you don't like this house, you don't have to take it. You can get yourself a house anywhere in Memphis. Do you like it?'

"I told him, 'I love it.' I'm crazy about the kitchen. It's got a real large kitchen, but I love this whole house."

Among the other things that Elvis loved were Mary Jenkins's collard greens and corn bread. "Sometimes he would want collard greens. 'I just want collard greens and corn bread,' he would tell me, and I'd fix 'em and I'd cut him a big bowl of onions and set it on a tray, and he would enjoy that."

Elvis expressed his gratitude to Mary with kind words as well as with the gifts he gave to his favorite cook. "He would say, 'Mary, that's really good.'

"One time his friend Lamar Fike said, 'Elvis, you just got to eat some of Mary's egg pie. You just got to.' Elvis said, 'Lamar, if anybody knows if Mary can cook, you know I know, but I'm full. Mary can cook,

Mary Jenkins

but I just don't want nothing to eat.'" Mary laughs while retelling the tale.

Another of her amusing anecdotes concerns Elvis's disappointment over Chicago hamburgers. "He ate lots of hamburgers and cheeseburgers," she recalls. "He was crazy about them. He said to his cousin Billy, 'Billy, you ought to eat one of these hamburgers of Mary's. These are the best hamburgers in the world.'"

Mary remembers that Elvis added, "'Mary, if I go back to Chicago I'm taking you with me. They are some of the poorest cooks I ever seen.'"

She laughs, remembering, "Elvis called the police [in Chicago] to see if they would go and find him some good hamburgers. They brought him some back that he said were even worse than they had in the motel."

As for one other grand favorite of the Presley palate there's the famed fried peanut butter and banana sandwich. Mary has no idea how many of them she must have prepared over the years.

"Oh," she says, "When he started on that fried peanut butter and banana sandwich…whenever he called, that was what he wanted. That started I guess a little along 1975. They are good. You toast your bread first and spread your peanut butter on your bread. Slice your bananas and put 'em on there. Put on your skillet on low heat and turn that sandwich from side to side with your spatula until it gets warm all the way through."

And there you go—Elvis's personal favorite sandwich.

Priscilla was partial to Mary's tuna fish salad,

while both Priscilla and Lisa Marie doted on her fried corn.

"Her and Priscilla was both crazy about my fried corn," says Mary. "Priscilla said she tried and tried to fix it and messed up about ten different times trying to make her corn like I tried to tell her to fix it," says Mary with a warm laugh.

"Lisa liked vegetables, but specially my fried corn. I asked her, 'Lisa, what you gonna have for breakfast?'

" 'Some of that corn you cooked last night.'

"Baby, I ain't got no more corn here. It's gone.'

"'Well, can't you get some?'

"Oh, yes, I'd get her some more and fix it for her."

Mary adds, "When Lisa was little, she loved French fries and macaroni and cheese in the box. She loved that. She'd have her little friends over and that's all we'd have to fix."

Near Christmas every year is when memories of Elvis lay closest on Mary's mind.

"He would come in on December 14 for Christmas. This time of year is real sad feeling for me. We would be so used to him coming in. He was wonderful, a wonderful person. A really nice, sweet person," says Mary Jenkins, the Graceland cook with the golden touch.

★ COME WHAT MAY CORN CHOWDER ★

2 cups water
2 cups potatoes, diced
½ onion, chopped
4 ribs celery, diced
¾ teaspoon basil
1 bay leaf
1 17-ounce can cream-style corn
2 cups skim milk
1 cup chopped fresh tomatoes
 Salt and white pepper to taste
½ cup grated Cheddar cheese

In a big stock pot combine the water, potatoes, onion, celery, basil, and bay leaf. Bring the liquid to a boil. Simmer until the potatoes are tender.

Remove the bay leaf and add the corn, milk, and tomatoes. Heat thoroughly, but do not boil! Add the salt, pepper, and cheese, stirring until the cheese melts and the soup thickens.

Serves 8.

Linda Kent
Elvis Country Fan Club

Salads and Dressings

★ VIVA LAS VEGAS VINAIGRETTE ★

⅓   cup red wine vinegar
⅔   cup virgin olive oil (cold-pressed)
2   cloves garlic, cut into 4 pieces
1   to 3 tablespoons French-style mustard
1   tablespoon soy sauce

In a jar combine all of the ingredients. Put the top on snugly and shake.

The dressing tastes better when the garlic has had a couple of hours to soak in the vinegar. I usually start with just the vinegar and garlic and then add the other ingredients a few hours later.

The vinaigrette keeps well. Store it in a cool, dry place (not the refrigerator). It does well in a closed cupboard. Just shake before using.

If you are a big olive oil fan, you may wish to make the proportions ¼ cup vinegar and ¾ cup olive oil.

Serves 4 to 6.

Judith Murray
Toronto, Ontario

★ SANTA LUCIA SALAD DRESSING ★

¼   cup apple cider vinegar
1   cup cooking oil or olive oil
1   teaspoon mustard
½   cup sugar

In a blender combine all of the ingredients and blend thoroughly until the sugar is dissolved and the mixture has thickened. Transfer to a container with an airtight lid and refrigerate until needed.

Serves 4 to 6.

Edie Hand
Cousin of Elvis Presley

★ SPANISH EYES SPINACH WITH CREAMY ★ YOGURT DRESSING

1   16-ounce bag fresh spinach

Dressing:
⅔   cup olive oil
½   cup plain or strawberry yogurt
2   tablespoons lemon juice, bottled or freshly squeezed
1   tablespoon white wine vinegar
2   tablespoons French-style mustard
2   tablespoons honey

Suggested Toppings:
Bacon bits or bacon pieces
Slivered almonds
Mandarin oranges, fresh or drained from a can
Croutons

Clean the spinach and break it into bite-sized pieces. Spin dry if possible to fully clean off the sand and grit.

In a medium bowl combine the olive oil, yogurt, lemon juice, vinegar, mustard, and honey, and whip with a hand mixer on medium speed for about 1 minute. Pour the salad dressing mixture over the fresh spinach to coat. Garnish with the toppings of your choice.
Serves 4 to 6.

Rose-Ann Bernett
Canadian National Elvis Tribute Fan Club

WHEN ELVIS WAS A YOUNGSTER, HE WOULD VISIT HIS GRANDMOTHER DODGER'S HOUSE WHERE HE INSISTED ON EATING OUT OF THE SAME DISHES AT EVERY MEAL. SO GRANDMA DODGER DESIGNATED SPECIFIC DISHES FOR ELVIS AND KEPT THEM IN THEIR OWN CORNER OF THE CABINET.

★ BAREFOOT BALLAD ★ BROCCOLI CAULIFLOWER SALAD

1	head broccoli, cut into florets
1	head cauliflower, broken into florets
1	onion, peeled and chopped
2	cups mayonnaise
1	cup sour cream
2	tablespoons white vinegar
2	tablespoons sugar
	Dash steak seasoning sauce
	Dash hot pepper sauce
	Salt and pepper to taste

In a large salad bowl mix the broccoli, cauliflower, and onion together. In a separate bowl mix together a dressing out of the remaining ingredients. Pour the dressing over the vegetables. Toss well and chill for several hours or overnight. Toss again before serving.
Serves 8.

Linda Kent
Elvis Country Fan Club

Elvis enjoys a visit with three of his favorite "girls," wife Priscilla, grandmother Dodger, and daughter Lisa Marie.

★ SHOUT IT OUT VEGETABLE SALAD ★

1	cup sugar
½	cup oil
1	teaspoon salt
3¼	cups vinegar
½	teaspoon pepper
1	teaspoon bean juice
½	cup chopped parsley
1	green bell pepper, chopped
1	15-ounce can French-style green beans
1	15-ounce can white shoe peg corn
1	4-ounce jar pimientos
½	cup chopped purple onion
1	15-ounce can tiny green peas

In a small saucepan bring the sugar, oil, salt, vinegar, pepper, and bean juice to a boil. Let the mixture stand to cool.

In a separate mixing bowl mix together all of the vegetables, adding the peas last. Pour the liquid mixture over the vegetables. Refrigerate overnight.

Serves 6.

Mary Tom Speer Reid
The Speer Family

Courtesy of the Speer Family

Members of gospel music's famed Speer Family gathering around the piano in this photograph from the early 1950s are: Rosa Nell Speer Powell at the piano; back row (left to right): Ben Speer, Lena (Mom) Speer, Mary Tom Speer Reid, G. T. (Dad) Speer, and Brock Speer. The Speers are recipients of numerous Dove Awards from the Gospel Music Association and were friends of Elvis.

★ TRUE LOVE TOMATOES WITH TARRAGON ★ VINEGAR AND BASIL SALAD

1¼ cups tarragon vinegar
1¼ cups water
½   teaspoon dried basil
1   teaspoon salt
2   teaspoon sugar
    Pinch pepper
4   tomatoes, peeled and sliced

In a small bowl mix all of the ingredients except the tomatoes. Place the tomatoes in a flat, shallow pan. Pour the mixture over the tomatoes. Refrigerate for 30 minutes.
    Serves 4 to 6.

Sue Hacker Hardesty
Cousin of Elvis Presley

★ THERE'S ALWAYS ME THREE BEAN SALAD ★

2   16-ounce cans cut green beans
1   16-ounce can wax beans
1   16-ounce can red kidney beans
½   purple onion, sliced
⅔   cup oil
⅔   cup cider vinegar
⅓   cup sugar
1   teaspoon salt
½   teaspoon pepper
2   dashes dry mustard
¼   pound bacon, cooked

The day before you plan to serve the salad, drain the beans and place them in a glass bowl. Add the onion. In a separate bowl mix the oil, vinegar, sugar, salt, pepper, and mustard together. Pour over the bean mixture. Cover and refrigerate.
    Just before serving, crumble the bacon over the salad and toss.
    Serves 10.

Jean Busby
Elvis Country Fan Club

★ KATHY'S KILLA BASILICA ★

1	**head bibb lettuce**
2	**large ripe tomatoes, sliced ¼-inch thick**
	Salt
1	**medium bunch fresh basil**
2	**large fresh mozzarella balls, sliced ¼-inch thick**
	Extra virgin olive oil
	Ground pepper

"Elvis loved his music, his friends, his mama, and last but not least he loved a good meal. If he would've had a chance to try Kathy's Killa Basilica, he would have been an instant fan!"—Tony Brown

Line a serving platter or 6 salad plates with lettuce. Arrange the tomato slices on the lettuce and sprinkle the tomatoes with salt. Place the basil leaves on the tomatoes and top with the sliced mozzarella. Drizzle with olive oil and season with the freshly ground pepper. **Serves 6.**

Tony Brown
President, MCA Records Nashville
and former musical accompanyist for Elvis Presley

Edie Hand and Donna Presley Early visit with Tony Brown in 1996.

★ BLACK STAR BLACK-EYED PEA SALAD ★

3	5-ounce cans black-eyed peas
1	15-ounce can carrots
1	cup onion, chopped
1	clove garlic, crushed
1	2-ounce jar sliced pimiento
1	10¼-ounce can tomato soup
3¼	cups sugar
3¼	cups white vinegar
5	tablespoons steak seasoning sauce
½	cup oil

Drain, wash, and dry the black-eyed peas. Place in a large bowl. Add the remaining ingredients, and mix well. Chill until ready to serve.
Serves 10.

Georgann Reynolds
Elvis Country Fan Club

★ LATEST FLAME HOT POTATO SALAD ★

6	medium potatoes
2	tablespoons bacon
2	tablespoons all-purpose flour
1	cup water
3	tablespoons cider vinegar
	Salt and pepper to taste
⅓	cup chopped parsley

In a big saucepan cook the potatoes in their jackets in a little water for about 20 minutes.

Drain. Peel, slice, and place the potatoes in a large bowl. Fry the bacon and remove from the pan. Let the bacon drain on a paper towel. Add the flour to the bacon drippings in the pan, mix, and cook for 1 minute. Gradually add the water and stir. Stir in the vinegar and the salt and pepper, cook for 1 minute. Pour the sauce over the potatoes, and sprinkle with crumbled bacon and parsley.
Serves 6.

Lela Hacker
Cousin of Elvis Presley

Ronnie McDowell's Career Pays Homage to "The King"

Singer, songwriter, and Tennessee boy Ronnie McDowell first felt the impact of Elvis Presley when he was four years old. "It was about 1954, when I saw Elvis on Tommy and Jimmy Dorsey's *Stage Show* on TV. Instantly I became his biggest fan. Elvis just had that thing, that whatever it is. I'm not sure anybody can describe it, but his voice was different," said McDowell. This assessment comes from the guy with the most uncanny vocal resemblance to Elvis.

In fact, McDowell is known as "the official voice of Graceland." "They say that. I don't know," he says modestly. But his credits speak as loudly as lyrics. After all his voice is the one that has filled in the vocals for most of the movies and TV shows about Elvis's life. Remember Kurt Russell in the 1979 TV movie *Elvis*? That was McDowell's voice you heard singing the thirty-six songs on the soundtrack. That goes ditto for *Elvis and the Beauty Queen, Elvis and Me,* the 1990 ABC-TV series *Elvis,* and about ten more films, including, most recently, *Elvis Meets Nixon.*

McDowell, a native of Fountain Head (near Portland), Tennessee, has had a solid career over the last twenty years as a tunesmith and hit singer, but he recognizes that he owes much of his success to Presley. His career zoomed sky high overnight in August 1977 after he co-wrote and recorded the tribute "The King Is Gone." The song sold a million copies in no time flat. "I was working in clubs and writing songs for a lot of artists in the early 1970s. Elvis was working and having hit records then. I had to perform whatever was Top 40, so if Elvis had a song called 'Burning Love' or 'Moody Blue' or whatever, I had to be able to perform it," McDowell recalled. "Whenever I was doing an Elvis song or Johnny Cash song, I would try to do it in their voices. I was at a club one night in Nashville, the Country Godfather, when a guy heard me do an Elvis song." The guy, the late Lee Morgan, was totally floored by McDowell's vocal similarity to Elvis. Then, within hours after Presley's death, the two wrote "The King Is Gone," and Morgan insisted that McDowell record it in his Elvis voice. "That's how it all came about," says McDowell. "It was all done on a shoestring budget. We kind of threw it together. I

went down the next day, got some acetates made, and took it around to radio stations myself. We had no earthly idea what we had."

The tune not only sold a million but it set McDowell's career off like a rocket. Over the next decade, McDowell took fourteen tunes into country's Top Ten charts, including such hits as "Wandering Eyes," "Older Women," "Personally," "You're Gonna Ruin My Bad Reputation," "New York Minute," "It's Only Make Believe," and "I Love You, I Love You, I Love You." And, in the summer of 1997, McDowell went into the studios to record *Elvis: A Tribute to the King,* a CD with nineteen Elvis Presley hits, with guitarist Scotty Moore, drummer D. J. Fontana, and the Jordanaires, the very musicians and singers that recorded with Elvis. "It was a fun project, something I always wanted to do," he says. "To work with those guys was a treat in itself, just working with and getting to know them. I wrote and recorded a song called 'Soulmates,' which is now on an album with songs by the Rolling Stones, Cheap Trick, and others." (The album, *All the King's Men,* was nominated for a Grammy.) "I would never have gotten to do it if not for Scotty Moore and D. J. Fontana. I did it because they're my heroes," he says.

But first there was Elvis. "Only one in a billion comes along with that charisma and talent and is born to do what he did. He was definitely a different kind of force in the business. He was not like Perry Como or Hank Williams or Lefty Frizzell. He was totally unique and different. He still stands out to this day," McDowell says of the phenomenon that was Elvis Presley. "Elvis came from those beginnings that he came from, and when he sang, he was pouring out his soul and his heart like nobody who had ever come down the pike. He wanted it so bad—to get out of what he had been in, for his parents and himself, and sometimes when you reach down in the pit of your soul, I think it reaches out to people and touches them. He did that in his voice. You listen to those early Sun Records. Do you hear anybody that has that kind of emotion and soul today? There was no false pretense or phoniness. He was real.

"There've been a lot of parallels between Elvis

and me. I don't know if they were meant to be or are just coincidental," says McDowell, "but I would not be where I'm at if not for Elvis.

"The first place I ever sang was aboard the *USS Hancock* in July 1968. Unbeknownst to me Elvis sang in that very spot on *The Milton Berle Show*."

Call it fate or destiny or whatever you will, McDowell's ability to mimic Elvis is so incredible that even Elvis's close friends and family members haven't been able to distinguish between the King's voice and McDowell's. And it was Priscilla Presley who requested that McDowell furnish the vocals for the Elvis movies. Even Elvis's fans have been touched by McDowell's talent. "I've got fans that have given me their entire Elvis Presley record collections," says the man with a voice like "the King."

Alan Mayor

Ronnie McDowell unveiled his hand-crafted sculpture of Elvis Presley at the 1996 International Country Music Fan Fair in Nashville. The statue, which took three years to complete, is made from cellu-clay. Ronnie entitled the statue Elvis '56 by Ronnie McDowell '96.

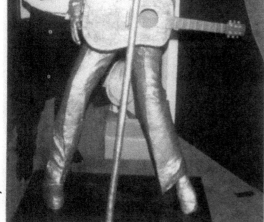

Alan Mayor

Guitar legend Scotty Moore (left) shows his pluck with the statue's guitar.

★ Ronnie's Corn Salad ★

2   **12-ounce cans Green Giant shoe peg corn, drained**
1   **box fresh cherry tomatoes, cut into quarters**
1   **green bell pepper, seeded and chopped**
1   **cucumber, peeled, seeded, and chopped**
½   **cup nonfat sour cream**
¼   **cup mayonnaise**
2   **tablespoons white vinegar**
½   **teaspoon celery seed**
1   **teaspoon dry mustard**
1   **teaspoon black pepper**
2   **teaspoons salt**

In a large nonmetallic bowl mix all the vegetables together. In a separate bowl combine the sour cream and the remaining ingredients. Pour over the vegetables and mix thoroughly. Cover and refrigerate overnight.

Serve with barbecue or hamburgers, or stuffed in a tomato.
Serves about 6.

Ronnie McDowell

Ronnie McDowell (far right) makes his performing debut aboard the USS Hancock in 1968. On stage with Ronnie are Chuck Nitchie (left) and Joe Hedreth. Ronnie learned years later that Elvis once performed aboard the same ship.

Ronnie McDowell (center) is flanked by (left to right) D. J. Fontana; Jordanaires Gordon Stoker, Neal Mathews, Duane West, and Ray Walker; and Scotty Moore.

★ SEPARATE WAYS SEVEN LAYER SALAD ★

2¼   cups chopped or torn lettuce
1½   cups chopped green onions
½   cup chopped bell peppers
½   cup chopped celery
1   16-ounce can small peas
6   boiled eggs, chopped
1½   cups mayonnaise or creamy Italian
        dressing
1½   cups grated cheese

In a large salad bowl place a layer of lettuce, and then layer the remaining ingredients on top, alternating each layer with lettuce.
Serves 6.

Brenda Morrow
Montgomery, Alabama

★ MARGUERITA MEDITERRANEAN ★ LAYERED SALAD

      Romaine or leaf lettuce or fresh
        spinach
1   bell pepper
1   bunch green onions
¼   large celery rib
1   16-ounce can sweet peas
1   8-ounce can ripe olives
2   cups mayonnaise
1   package Ranch or Italian salad mix
4   cups shredded Cheddar cheese
½   cup bacon bits

Chop the greens, bell pepper, onions (keep tops on), and celery and place each in a separate small bowl. Drain the sweet peas and olives and place each in a small bowl as well. Then layer the ingredients, one by one, in a 9 x 13-inch serving dish, starting with the greens.

In a small bowl mix the mayonnaise and dressing mix and pour evenly over the salad. Top with grated cheese and bacon bits. Cover and refrigerate overnight (a must).

If you want, you can substitute carrots, bean sprouts, or other vegetables, or add them to taste.
Serves 6.

Marva Kaye Ward
Elvis Country Fan Club

★ KING CREOLE KING CRAB PLATTER SALAD ★

1   8-ounce package Alaskan King Crab,
      thawed, or 1 7½-ounce can
      Alaskan king crab
1   pound fresh green beans
1   medium onion, thinly sliced
2   eggs, hard-cooked
1   cucumber, scored and sliced
1   tomato, cut into wedges
      Romaine lettuce
      Parsley

Oil and Vinegar Dressing:
½   cup olive oil
1¼   cups white wine vinegar
2   teaspoons chopped parsley
½   teaspoon garlic salt
      Dash white pepper

Drain and slice the crab meat. Steam the green beans. Slice the onion, eggs, cucumbers, and tomato. Place the crab on the lettuce in the center of the platter. Arrange the remaining ingredients around the crab and garnish with parsley.

In a small bowl combine the olive oil, white wine vinegar, parsley, garlic salt, and pepper. Mix well. Pour the oil and vinegar dressing over each serving.

Serves 4.

Anthony Hacker
Cousin of Elvis Presley

Elvis's Gold Albums

(Sales in excess of half a million copies)

Elvis Presley (1956)
Elvis (1956)
Loving You (1957)
King Creole (1958)
Elvis Is Back (1960)
Something for Everybody (1961)
Pot Luck (1962)
Girls! Girls! Girls! (1962)
It Happened at the World's Fair (1963)
Fun in Acapulco (1964)
Kissin' Cousins (1964)
Roustabout (1964)

Girl Happy (1965)
Elvis for Everyone (1965)
Harum Scarum (1965)
Paradise Hawaiian Style (1966)
Elvis Presley–NBC TV Special (1969)
From Elvis in Memphis (1969)
From Memphis to Vegas/From Vegas to Memphis (1969)
On Stage–February 1970 (1970)
Elvis: That's the Way It Is (1970)
Elvis Country (I'm 1000 Years Old) (1971)

This photo of Elvis was made while he was on leave from the Army.

★ Fun in Acapulco Salad ★

2	heads lettuce
2	tomatoes
2	5-ounce cans sliced ripe olives
1	avocado
1½	pounds Cheddar cheese, grated
2	10-ounce cans ranch-style beans, drained
1	12-ounce bottle French salad dressing
1	bag corn chips or tortilla chips

In a large salad bowl mix the lettuce, tomatoes, olives, avocado, and cheese. Mix the beans and dressing together in a separate bowl. Just before serving, add the bean mixture to the salad and place the chips on top.

Serves 6.

Georgann Reynolds
Elvis Country Fan Club

★ Pieces of My Life Pie Crust Salad ★

1	ready-made 9-inch pie crust
	Lettuce or Romaine leaves
½	cup sliced celery
1	8-ounce can sliced water chestnuts, drained
½	sweet red pepper, diced
1½	cups mayonnaise
3¼	teaspoon seasoned salt
1¼	cup sliced green onion
½	yellow pepper, diced
1	cup frozen peas, thawed and drained
¼	pound Cheddar cheese, shredded
3	hard-boiled eggs, chopped or shredded
1	tomato, cut into wedges
½	pound bacon, fried crisp and crumbled

Bake the pie crust according to the directions on the package. While the crust is baking, wash and pat the lettuce dry. Let the pie crust cool when done, then layer the lettuce inside it. Sprinkle with celery, chestnuts, and red pepper.

In a small bowl mix the mayonnaise with the seasoned salt. Blend well. Spread ¾ cup of the mayonnaise mixture over the celery, chestnuts, and red pepper. Sprinkle the green onion, yellow pepper, peas, and cheese over this. Spread the remaining mayonnaise over this layer. Garnish with eggs, adding the crumbled bacon around the edges of the pie crust. Then lay the tomato wedges next to the bacon around the crust.

Serves 6 to 8.

Phyllis M. Hopkins
Orlando, Florida
Elvis Presley Continentals of Florida

★ CARNY TOWN CORN BREAD SALAD ★

1   cup self-rising cornmeal
1   teaspoon all-purpose flour
½   cup (1 stick) margarine
2   eggs
1   8-ounce container sour cream

Topping:
1   cup chopped onion
1   cup chopped bell pepper
1   cup chopped fresh tomato
1   cup small peas, drained
1   cup cubed sweet pickles
1   cup mayonnaise
1   cup grated cheese
1   10-ounce bottle bacon bits

Preheat the oven to 400°. In a large bowl mix the cornmeal, flour, margarine, eggs, and sour cream together. Spoon into a greased baking dish and bake for 20 to 25 minutes. When done, crumble the corn bread into a salad bowl.

In a medium bowl mix the vegetables, mayonnaise, and cheese together. Spoon the vegetable topping over the crumbled corn bread. Sprinkle bacon bits over the top of the salad. Serve.

Serves 4 to 6.

Guy Blackburn
Red Bay, Alabama

Presley Tanita Tucker is the center of attention for her Elvis fan mom, country music star Tanya Tucker (right), and Elvis's cousin Edie Hand.

★ SATISFYING FROZEN FRUIT SALAD ★

1   cup chopped nuts

1   tablespoon chopped maraschino
       cherries

1   9-ounce can crushed pineapple,
       well drained

½   pint sour cream

1   cup sugar

2   tablespoons lemon juice

⅓   teaspoon salt

3   or 4 bananas, diced

In a large bowl combine all of the ingredients. Stir gently, but well. Spoon into 12 paper muffin tin liners. Freeze in the muffin tins. Remove the paper before serving.

     This is good served with turkey.
Makes 12.

Francine and Cecil Blackwood
The Blackwood Brothers

THE ASSEMBLIES OF GOD CHURCH PLAYED
A VITAL ROLE IN THE PRESLEY FAMILY WHEN
ELVIS WAS A BOY. RELIGION SO INSPIRED
YOUNG ELVIS THAT HIS AUNT NASH WOULD
REMEMBER HIM LAYING HIS HANDS ON HIS
MOTHER AND FATHER WHEN THEY WERE
SICK OR FEELING POORLY AND SAYING,
"JESUS WILL MAKE IT ALL BETTER."

★ FANTASTIC FRUIT SALAD DRESSING ★

½   cup sour cream

½   teaspoon ground ginger

1 ¼   teaspoons ground nutmeg

⅛   teaspoon salt

1   teaspoon lemon juice

1   teaspoon sugar

     Quart of fresh fruit (your choice)

In a small bowl mix the ingredients together well. Let stand for 10 minutes. Pour over a quart of fresh fruit: strawberries, blueberries, raspberries, or whatever else is in season.
Serves 4.

Debbie Lustrea Paustch
Wheaton, Illinois

★ TWENTY-FOUR-HOUR TROPICAL SALAD ★

1	**15-ounce can pineapple**
1	**11-ounce can mandarin oranges**
1	**cup flaked coconut**
½	**cup miniature marshmallows**
1	**8-ounce carton sour cream**

Put the pineapple and mandarin oranges together into a colander and drain. Remove them and cut into small pieces. In a salad bowl combine all of the ingredients together and mix. Cover with plastic wrap. Put into the refrigerator and chill overnight.

Serves 6.

Pat Early
Donna Presley Early's mother-in-law

Elvis's Leading Ladies (Part Two)

Match the actress to the film.

1. Ann-Margret	A. *Blue Hawaii*
2. Joan Blackman	B. *Change of Habit*
3. Michele Carey	C. *Flaming Star*
4. Barbara Eden	D. *Follow That Dream*
5. Shelley Fabares	E. *G.I. Blues*
6. Dolores Hart	F. *Girl Happy*
7. Anne Helm	G. *Girls! Girls! Girls!*
8. Marlyn Mason	H. *King Creole*
9. Mary Tyler Moore	I. *Live a Little, Love a Little*
10. Hope Lange	J. *Love Me Tender*
11. Debra Paget	K. *The Trouble With Girls*
12. Juliet Prowse	L. *Viva Las Vegas*
13. Stella Stevens	M. *Wild in the Country*

ANSWERS: 1. L, 2. A, 3. I, 4. C, 5. F, 6. H, 7. D, 8. K, 9. B, 10. M, 11. J, 12. E, 13. G

★ CRYING IN THE CHAPEL CRANBERRY SALAD ★

1	3-ounce package raspberry gelatin
1	cup hot water
1	15-ounce can whole cranberries
1	20-ounce can drained crushed pineapple
1	cup chopped apples

In a large bowl mix the gelatin and hot water together. Add the cranberries, pineapple, and apples. Pour into a mold and refrigerate overnight.

Serves 6.

Rick Stanley
Stepbrother of Elvis Presley

Courtesy of Rick Stanley

Elvis poses with a crew of friends and family. Among those pictured are Nancy Sinatra (far left), Elvis's father, Vernon, and his wife, Dee (third and fourth from left), and Dee's son, Rick (in the middle).

★ ARE YOU LONESOME TONIGHT ★
ORANGE SALAD

1   11-ounce can Mandarin orange
     slices, drained
1   8-ounce can pineapple chunks,
     drained
1   16-ounce container cottage cheese
1   12-ounce container nondairy
     whipped topping
1   3-ounce package orange gelatin

In a nonmetallic bowl stir all of the ingredients together. Refrigerate and enjoy.

Sandi and Willie Wynn

Willie Wynn (wearing sunglasses) knew Elvis when Willie was a member of the Oak Ridge Boys band. Also pictured in this 1973 photo of the Oak Ridge Boys are (clockwise from far left) band members William Lee Golden, Richard Sterban, Duane Allen, Mark Ellerbe, Don Breland, Tony Brown, and John Rich. Tony Brown, who went on to become one of Nashville's most respected record producers, also played keyboards with Elvis.

★ ROCK A HULA BABY ORANGE TROPICS SALAD ★

2	11-ounce cans mandarin oranges, drained
1	20-ounce can crushed pineapple, drained
1	16-ounce container sour cream
2	3-ounce boxes orange gelatin
1	10½-ounce bag miniature marshmallows
1	8-ounce container nondairy whipped topping

In a large mixing bowl combine the oranges, pineapple, and sour cream. Add the gelatin. Stir all together well. Add the whipped topping and marshmallows. Mix together and refrigerate.

Serves 6.

Rhea Marie Edenfield
President; Elvis, Forever and Always

★ WONDERFUL CHICKEN SALAD ★

1	whole chicken, cooked or 4 to 6 chicken breasts, poached lightly until done, but not boiled
1½	cups diced celery
2	tablespoons finely chopped parsley
1¼	cups almonds, finely chopped
	Salt and pepper to taste
½	cup heavy cream, whipped and not sweetened
1	cup mayonnaise
1½	tablespoons lemon juice, fresh squeezed

After cooking the chicken, remove the skin and bones while still warm. (It's easier that way.) Discard the skin and bones. Cut the chicken into bite-sized pieces.

In a large bowl combine the chicken, celery, parsley, and almonds. Season with salt and pepper to taste. In a small bowl mix the whipping cream and mayonnaise together and add to the chicken mixture. Sprinkle the lemon juice on at the very last and toss thoroughly, but gently. Serve at once. Makes a nice luncheon dish.

Serves 4.

Cecil Blackwood
The Blackwood Brothers

Breads and Company

★ SOUTHERN CORN BREAD ★

1 cup self-rising flour
1 cup yellow cornmeal
½ teaspoon salt
3 teaspoons baking powder
1 tablespoon sugar
1 cup milk
1 egg
2 tablespoons bacon drippings

Preheat the oven to 375°. In a large bowl mix together the flour, cornmeal, salt, baking powder, and sugar. In a separate bowl beat the egg. Add the eggs to the milk. Combine the 2 mixtures and stir well. In an 8-inch square baking pan melt the bacon drippings. Add the melted drippings to the batter and stir. Pour the mixture into the baking pan and bake for 20 minutes.
Serves about 10.

Sue Hacker Hardesty
Cousin of Elvis Presley

★ KISS ME QUICK CRACKLIN' CORN BREAD ★

1 cup self-rising cornmeal
1 cup buttermilk
1 cup pork cracklin's
½ cup self-rising flour
½ cup vegetable oil

Preheat the oven to 450°. In a large mixing bowl combine the cornmeal, buttermilk, cracklin's, flour, and ¼ cup of oil. In an 8-inch skillet heat 4 tablespoons of oil until it is very hot. Pour the batter into the skillet. Bake for 20 minutes or until golden brown, slice, and serve warm. Add a glass of hot tea and sliced onions and get set for the best 10 minutes of eating you'll do in the South!
Serves 8 to 10.

Jackie Hacker Coleman
Cousin of Elvis Presley

★ CATCHIN' ON FAST COUNTRY CORN BREAD ★

1	cup yellow cornmeal
1	cup self-rising flour
¼	cup sugar
4	teaspoons baking powder
½	teaspoon salt
¼	cup (½ stick) butter or shortening, softened
1	cup buttermilk (or whole milk)
1	egg

Preheat the oven to 425°. In a big bowl blend the cornmeal, flour, sugar, baking powder, and salt together. Add the butter or shortening and stir until well blended. Add the milk and egg and stir until the mixture is completely moist (it will be a little lumpy). Pour into a greased 9-inch iron skillet. Bake for 20 minutes, until golden brown on top. You can also pour the batter into a greased iron corn sticks mold and bake about 15 minutes until golden brown.

Serves 8 to 10.

Jill McQuown
Memphis, Tennessee

★ ELVIS'S FAVORITE CORN BREAD ★

1	teaspoon oil
2	cups cornmeal
1	cup all-purpose flour
1	tablespoon baking powder
1½	tablespoons sugar
2½	cups buttermilk
3	eggs
¼	cup oil

In a skillet sprinkle 1 teaspoon of oil and a little of the meal and heat. Mix the remaining ingredients together and pour into the skillet. Cook until golden brown.

Serves 4 to 6.

Mary Jenkins
Personal cook for Elvis Presley

★ FAME AND FORTUNE ★ OLD-FASHIONED CORN BREAD

3 cups self-rising cornmeal
1 cup self-rising flour
2 teaspoons baking powder (optional)
2 teaspoons sugar (optional)
3 eggs
4 cups buttermilk
⅔ cup bacon drippings (cooled) or vegetable oil

Preheat the oven to 400°. In a large mixing bowl sift together all of the dry ingredients. Beat the eggs and add the buttermilk, bacon drippings, and oil. Add the egg mixture to the dry mixture and stir well. Pour the mixture into muffin tins, a regular loaf pan, or a preheated cast-iron skillet. (To preheat the skillet, pour a small amount of oil into the skillet and place it in the oven until hot.) Bake until golden brown, about 15 to 20 minutes in muffin tins, or about 35 to 40 minutes in larger pans.

Serves about 10.

Betty Jo McMichael
Co-owner, Whistle Stop Cafe
Irondale, Alabama

Elvis's father Vernon enjoys the best seat in the house while watching his son perform.

★ LOVING YOU LOW-FAT BUTTERMILK ★ CORN BREAD

2	cups self-rising cornmeal
2	tablespoons vegetable oil
1½	cups buttermilk
1	egg

Preheat the oven to 475°. In a bowl combine the cornmeal, oil, buttermilk, and egg, and mix well. Pour a small amount of additional oil into a cast-iron skillet. Preheat the skillet in the hot oven. Sprinkle a small amount of cornmeal over the bottom of the skillet. Pour in the cornmeal batter. Bake for 15 to 20 minutes or until golden brown. **Serves about 10.**

Bill McMichael
Co-owner, Whistle Stop Cafe
Irondale, Alabama

Who Was He and What Did He Do? (Part One)

Match the film to Elvis's character and to his occupation.

1.	*Blue Hawaii*	A.	Pacer Burton	A.	Carnival hand
2.	*Charro!*	B.	Mike Edwards	B.	Delivery driver/honky-tonk singer
3.	*Double Trouble*	C.	Vince Everett	C.	Half-breed cowboy
4.	*Flaming Star*	D.	Chad Gates	D.	Farmer
5.	*Frankie & Johnny*	E.	Steve Grayson	E.	Impresario
6.	*G.I. Blues*	F.	Walter Gulick	F.	Army private
7.	*Harum Scarum*	G.	Walter Hale	G.	Mechanic/boxer
8.	*It Happened at the World's Fair*	H.	Johnny	H.	Movie star
9.	*Jailhouse Rock*	I.	Guy Lambert	I.	Pilot
10.	*Kid Galahad*	J.	Tulsa McLean	J.	Outlaw/cowboy
11.	*Love Me Tender*	K.	Clint Reno	K.	Rock musician
12.	*Loving You*	L.	Deke Rivers	L.	Recording artist
13.	*Roustabout*	M.	Charlie Rogers	M.	Singer/gambler
14.	*Speedway*	N.	Glenn Tyler	N.	Writer
15.	*The Trouble With Girls*	O.	Johnny Tyrone	O.	Tour guide
16.	*Wild in the Country*	P.	Jess Wade	P.	Stock car driver

ANSWERS: 1. D, O; 2. P, J; 3. I, K; 4. A, C; 5. H, M; 6. J, F; 7. O, H; 8. B, B; 9. C, L; 10. F, G; 11. K, D; 12. L, B; 13. M, A; 14. E, P; 15. G, E; 16. N, N

★ BIG BOSS MAN BUTTERMILK BISCUITS ★

2 cups self-rising flour
1½ teaspoons baking powder
2 teaspoons sugar
¼ cup vegetable oil
¾ to 1 cup buttermilk
   Melted butter or margarine
      (optional)

Preheat the oven to 450°. In a large mixing bowl combine the flour, baking powder and sugar. Stir well, raking the flour up the sides of the bowl to form a well. Pour the oil and the buttermilk into the well, and gently stir the flour into the liquids. Mix until the flour is completely blended with the liquids. The dough should be moist but not sticky.

Turn out the dough onto a floured surface and knead several times. Roll out the dough to ½-inch thickness and cut with biscuit cutter.

Place the biscuits on a lightly greased baking sheet. Bake for 12 to 15 minutes or until lightly brown. Brush with melted butter or margarine if desired.

Serves about 10.

Betty Jo McMichael
Co-owner, Whistle Stop Cafe
Irondale, Alabama

The Karate King poses with his father, Vernon, and Vernon's second wife, Dee, and Linda Thompson, Elvis's longtime girlfriend, at a martial arts demonstration.

★ GRANDMOTHER'S BUTTERMILK BISCUITS ★ WITH CHOCOLATE GRAVY

2 cups self-rising flour
1½ teaspoons baking powder
¼ teaspoon baking soda
1 teaspoon sugar
½ cup shortening
1 cup buttermilk

Chocolate Gravy:
2 tablespoons cocoa
1½ cups sugar
2 tablespoons all-purpose flour
1 teaspoon vanilla extract
3 cups water

This is my grandmother Hacker's recipe. She raised her twelve children on these delicious biscuits for breakfast.

— Edie Hand

Preheat the oven to 450°. In a large bowl combine the flour, baking powder, soda, and sugar. Cut in the shortening with a pastry blender or two knives. Add the buttermilk and knead until smooth and pliable. Roll the dough out on a floured surface to the desired thickness or about ½ inch. Cut with a biscuit cutter and place in a baking pan. Bake for about 12 minutes or until brown on top.

In a saucepan combine the cocoa, sugar, flour, vanilla, and water, and cook over medium heat until it boils. The mixture will slowly thicken. Cook for about 10 minutes. Pour over buttered hot biscuits. **Serves 10.**

Alice Hood Hacker
Niece of Elvis Presley's grandmother Minnie Mae Hood Presley

WHEN HE WAS TEN, IN 1945, ELVIS SANG AT THE ANNUAL MISSISSIPPI ALABAMA FAIR IN TUPELO. HE PERFORMED "OLD SHEP" AND CLAIMED SECOND PLACE. THE FIRST-PLACE WINNER WAS A SIX-YEAR-OLD GIRL WHO WARBLED "SENTIMENTAL JOURNEY."

★ POPPY SEED BISCUITS ★

1   **8-ounce package refrigerator biscuits**

3   **tablespoons butter, melted**
      Poppy seeds

Preheat the oven to 400°. Cut the biscuits in half; dip in melted butter. Place 3 halves cut side down around the edge of each muffin cup. Place one additional half in the center. Sprinkle with poppy seeds and bake for about 12 to 15 minutes or until golden brown.

Serve with additional butter.

Makes 6.

Varnes Hacker Humphries
Cousin of Elvis Presley

★ FAMILY RECIPE BUTTERMILK BISCUITS ★

5   **cups self-rising flour (Gold Medal or Martha White)**

1   **teaspoon baking soda**

8   **teaspoons sugar**

½   **teaspoon salt**

¼   **cup lukewarm water**

1   **¼-ounce envelope yeast**

1   **cup Crisco or other shortening**

2   **cups buttermilk**

In a large bowl mix together the flour, soda, sugar, and salt. Dissolve the yeast in the lukewarm water. Add the yeast mixture, shortening, and buttermilk to the flour mixture. Mix together well. Cover and let rise. Knead just a little. Refrigerate overnight.

When ready to bake, preheat the oven to 425°. Take out the amount needed and roll out to about ½-inch thickness on a floured surface with a floured rolling pin. Cut with a biscuit cutter and place the biscuits on a greased baking sheet. Bake for about 15 minutes or until golden. Serve piping hot and with lots of butter (the way Elvis liked them). The dough will keep in the refrigerator for 2 weeks, so you can have biscuits every day!

Makes about 2 dozen biscuits.

Minnie Mae Hood Presley
(as adapted by Alice Hood Hacker)
Grandmother of Elvis (and her niece)

★ GOLDEN COINS CHEESE GARLIC BISCUITS ★

2	**cups packaged biscuit mix**
⅔	**cup milk**
½	**cup shredded Cheddar cheese**
¼	**cup (½ stick) margarine or butter, melted**
¼	**teaspoon garlic powder**

Preheat the oven to 450°. In a large mixing bowl mix the biscuit mix, milk, and cheese until a soft dough forms. Beat vigorously for 30 seconds. Drop the dough by spoonfuls onto an ungreased cookie sheet. Bake for 8 to 10 minutes or until golden brown.

In a small bowl mix the margarine or butter and garlic powder, and brush over the warm biscuits before they are removed from the cookie sheet. Serve warm.

Makes a dozen.

Verna Melohn
Elvis fan

SEA OF LOVE—Elvis enjoyed nothing more than to be among his fans.

★ BILLY'S ORIGINAL HUSH PUPPIES RECIPE ★

1   cup self-rising flour
2   cups self-rising cornmeal
3   tablespoons sugar
1½   tablespoons baking powder
¼   cup oil
2   eggs, beaten
1   large onion, finely chopped
1   jalapeño pepper, finely chopped or
        ground in food processor
1   cup buttermilk

In a large bowl combine the flour, cornmeal, sugar, and baking powder and mix well. In a separate bowl combine the oil, eggs, onion, jalapeño pepper, and buttermilk, stirring well. Add the liquid mixture to the dry mixture and mix well. The batter will be stiff. Drop 2 tablespoons of batter for each hush puppy into the hot oil and fry for about 4 minutes or until brown.

Makes 10 to 12.

Bill McMichael
Co-owner, Whistle Stop Cafe
Irondale, Alabama

Elvis and members of his Army unit are seen here during their service in Germany.
Photo by Elvis's sergeant.

★ HOUND DOG HOMEMADE HUSH PUPPIES ★

1   **quart water**
1   **tablespoon salt**
1⅓   **tablespoons sugar**
1½   **tablespoons garlic**
2¼   **teaspoons granulated onion**
1   **pound yellow cornmeal**
     Oil for frying

In a large pot combine the water, salt, sugar, garlic, and onion. Bring to a rolling boil, then turn the flame off, and stir in the cornmeal. The mush will be very stiff—so stiff that it is difficult to stir. When fully mixed together, scrape the mush into a 9 x 13-inch pan, flatten on top, and allow it to cool. Later, if a skin has formed on top, peel it off and discard it. Knead the mush until pliable and easy to work with. Pinch off whatever size pieces you want the hush puppies to be and form them by hand just as you would do with modeling clay.

Deep-fry at 350° until hard on the outside. Do not put too many in the fryer at once because the oil will get too cool.

Makes 12 to 24 hush puppies, depending on the size.

Debbie Busby
Elvis Country Fan Club

Elvis and an Army buddy in Germany.
Photo by Elvis's sergeant.

★ LONESOME COWBOY'S SALLY LUNN BREAD ★

1	cake yeast
¼	cup warm water
2	eggs
2	cups warm milk
1	teaspoon salt
2	tablespoons sugar
¼	cup shortening, melted
4	cups all-purpose flour
	Butter

Preheat the oven to 450°. In a bowl dissolve the yeast in the warm water. In a separate bowl break the eggs and then add the milk, salt, sugar, and shortening. Thoroughly mix in the flour, add the yeast, and stir. Pour the batter into 2 well-greased loaf pans and let rise until double in size.

Bake for 30 to 45 minutes.

Serve by breaking—never cutting. Smooth on butter.

Makes about 12 pieces.

Jo Anne Phillips
Elvis Country Fan Club

★ SPEEDWAY SPOON BREAD ★

1	cup stone-ground yellow cornmeal
2	tablespoons shortening
3	13-ounce cans evaporated milk
4	eggs, beaten
1½	teaspoons salt
1	tablespoon baking powder

Preheat the oven to 450°. In a large saucepan boil the cornmeal, shortening, and 2 cans of the evaporated milk over medium heat, stirring constantly. Remove the pan from the heat and add the eggs, remaining can of evaporated milk, and salt. Quickly stir in the baking powder and pour into a greased 2-quart baking dish. Bake for 30 minutes.

Serves 8 to 10.

Linda Sue Hacker Whitaker
Cousin of Elvis Presley

★ TEXAS COFFEE CAKE ★

1   cup (2 sticks) butter

2   cups sugar

2   eggs

2   cups all-purpose flour

¼   teaspoon salt

1   teaspoon baking powder

1   8-ounce carton sour cream

½   teaspoon vanilla extract

Topping:

½   teaspoon ground cinnamon

1   cup chopped pecans

2   tablespoons sugar

Preheat the oven to 350°. Cream the butter, sugar, and eggs. Sift the flour, salt, and baking powder. Add to the butter mixture. Add the sour cream and vanilla. Beat for 4 to 5 minutes. Pour half of the batter into a greased and floured bundt pan.

In a small bowl combine the cinnamon, pecans, and sugar, and sprinkle half of the topping on top of the batter. Spread the remaining batter on top, and then the remaining topping. Bake for 45 minutes.

Serves 10.

Terry Blackwood
Former member of The Imperials, who sang backup for Elvis

★ TOO MUCH MONKEY BUSINESS ★
BANANA BREAD

1   cup sugar

⅓   cup margarine or butter, softened

2   eggs

1½ cups mashed ripe bananas (3 to 4 medium)

⅓   cup water

1⅔ cups all-purpose flour

1   teaspoon baking soda

½   teaspoon salt

¼   teaspoon baking powder

½   cup chopped nuts

Preheat the oven to 350°. Grease the bottom of a loaf pan. In a 2½-quart bowl mix the sugar and margarine. Stir in the eggs until well blended. Add the bananas and water and beat for 30 seconds. Stir in the remaining ingredients except for the nuts until moistened. Then stir in the nuts. Pour the batter into the pan and bake until a wooden pick inserted in the center comes out clean. For an 8-inch loaf pan, bake for 1 hour and 15 minutes or for a 9-inch pan, bake for 55 to 60 minutes. Cool 15 minutes. Loosen the sides of the loaf from the pan. Remove from the pan and cool completely before slicing.

Makes 1 loaf.

Marlene L. Nunez
Elvis Country Fan Club

★ LOVELY MANGO (OR BANANA) BREAD ★

2½ cups all-purpose flour
2 cups sugar
1 teaspoon salt
2 tablespoons baking soda
1 cup (2 sticks) butter or margarine,
    melted
2 cups mashed mangos or bananas
4 eggs, beaten

Preheat the oven to 350°. In a large bowl mix the flour, sugar, salt, and baking soda. Add the butter or margarine, and then add the mangos or bananas and the eggs. Mix well. Pour the batter into a loaf pan. Bake for 50 to 60 minutes.

Cool and then slice to eat. It's delicious!

Lovely Penaroza Kwock
Honolulu, Hawaii

Lovely Penaroza Kwock has been called "the greatest Elvis fan of them all." She met Elvis numerous times during his visits to Hawaii. She also sent him more than 7,000 letters between 1955 and 1977. (He responded to many of them.)

This picture of Vernon Presley was taken as he drove out of the gates of Graceland in September 1976.

★ BIKINI MOVIE ZUCCHINI BREAD ★

2½   cups all-purpose flour (all white or
        half white and half whole wheat)
¼   cup powdered milk
½   cup wheat germ
2   teaspoons baking soda
½   teaspoon baking powder
1   cup sugar
1   cup firmly packed brown sugar
3   teaspoons ground cinnamon
½   teaspoon ground nutmeg
1   cup oil
3   eggs, beaten
3   teaspoons vanilla extract
1   cup chopped nuts
2   cups peeled and grated zucchini

Preheat the oven to 350°. In a large mixing bowl combine all of the ingredients. Pour the batter into 2 well-greased loaf pans. Bake for 1 hour.

Makes 2 loaves.

Charlotte Myrick
Cousin of Elvis Presley

★ TEDDY BEER BREAD ★

3   cups self-rising flour
2   tablespoons sugar
1   12-ounce bottle beer
    Butter

Preheat the oven to 375°. In a large mixing bowl combine the flour and sugar. Pour in your favorite beer. As the mixture foams, stir the ingredients together to form a dough. Place the dough in a greased bread pan. Bake for an hour. When the loaf is done, turn it out and brush with butter.

Makes 1 loaf.

Shirley Beattie
Presley-Ites Fan Club
Orlando, Florida

★ PEACE IN THE VALLEY ★ PEANUT BUTTER BREAD

1¾ cups sifted all-purpose flour
2   teaspoons baking powder
¼   teaspoon baking soda
½   teaspoon salt
⅓   cup shortening
¾   cup peanut butter
⅔   cup sugar
2   eggs, slightly beaten
1   cup mashed ripe bananas

Preheat the oven to 350°. In a medium bowl sift the dry ingredients together. In a large bowl cream the shortening and peanut butter. Add the sugar gradually. Add the dry ingredients and mix until light and fluffy. Add the eggs and beat well. Stir in the dry ingredients alternately with the bananas. Do not beat. Spoon into a greased 5 x 9-inch loaf pan. Bake for 50 to 60 minutes.

Makes 1 loaf.

Judy Coleman Martino
Cousin of Elvis Presley

Elvis cradles a young fan.

★ KISMET KICHEL ★

3   **eggs**
1   **tablespoon sugar**
1   **tablespoon oil**
¼   **teaspoon salt**
     About 2 cups all-purpose flour
       (enough to make the dough easy
       to handle)
     Sugar for sprinkling

Preheat the oven to 400°. In a large bowl combine all of the ingredients. Turn onto a floured board. Roll as thinly as possible and cut into squares. Place on a well-greased cookie sheet. Sprinkle with sugar. Bake for 6 to 7 minutes.

Makes about 2 dozen pieces.

Kathy Ferguson
Presley-Ites Fan Club
Orlando, Florida

Elvis having a meal while stationed in Germany.

★ PUCKER UP AND GRIN SANDWICH ★

2	slices whole wheat bread (or white)
2	teaspoons good mayonnaise
2	whole dill pickles

Spread the mayonnaise on one side of each piece of bread. Thinly slice each pickle thin and place on one of the bread slices. Put the other slice of bread on top. Then just chomp, chew, and "pucker and grin." Wow!

Sue Sutherland
Haleyville, Alabama
"If I Can Dream"—Elvis In Alabama Fan Club

Who Was He and What Did He Do? (Part Two)

Match the film to Elvis's character and to his occupation.

1.	*Change of Habit*	A.	Lonnie Beale	A.	Army lieutenant/country boy
2.	*Clambake*	B.	John Carpenter	B.	Chaperone
3.	*Easy Come, Easy Go*	C.	Ross Carpenter	C.	Copter pilot
4.	*Follow That Dream*	D.	Danny Fisher	D.	Doctor
5.	*Fun in Acapulco*	E.	Scott Heyward	E.	Deep-sea fishing guide
6.	*Girl Happy*	F.	Lucky Jackson	F.	Frogman
7.	*Girls! Girls! Girls!*	G.	Ted Jackson	G.	Homesteader
8.	*King Creole*	H.	Toby Kwemper	H.	Acrobat/lifeguard
9.	*Kissin' Cousins*	I.	Joe Lightcloud	I.	Mill sweeper/night club singer
10.	*Live a Little, Love a Little*	J.	Mike McCoy	J.	Photographer
11.	*Paradise, Hawaiian Style*	K.	Greg Nolan	K.	Race driver
12.	*Spinout*	L.	Greg Richards	L.	Rancher
13.	*Stay Away, Joe*	M.	Josh Morgan & Jody Tatum	M.	Rodeo cowboy
14.	*Tickle Me*	N.	Rusty Wells	N.	Mechanic/Grand Prix driver
15.	*Viva Las Vegas*	O.	Mike Windgren	O.	Speedboat Racer

ANSWERS: 1. B, D; 2. E, O; 3. G, F; 4. H, G; 5. O, H; 6. N, B; 7. C, E; 8. D, I; 9. M, A; 10. K, J; 11. C, L; 12. J, K; 13. L, L; 14. A, M; 15. F, N

★ FRIED PEANUT BUTTER AND BANANA ★ SANDWICH

2   slices white bread
2   to 3 tablespoons smooth peanut
       butter
½   large, well-ripened banana, mashed
1   to 2 tablespoons margarine

An Elvis favorite at home.

This is how Elvis would have this treat: Spread the peanut butter on one side of both pieces of bread. Spread the mashed banana on top of the peanut butter on one of the bread slices. Put the two slices together to make a sandwich. In a skillet over medium heat, melt the margarine. When the margarine is hot, fry the sandwich, browning both sides. Serve and eat immediately.

Elvis usually ate his with a knife and fork.
Makes 1.

Donna Presley Early
First cousin of Elvis Presley

Vernon Presley is seen here behind the wheel of his El Camino at the Circle G ranch in Walls, Mississippi, about a half an hour's drive from Graceland.
(The "G" in Circle G stood for Graceland.)

★ EARLY MORNIN' RAIN ★ SPICY MANDARIN MUFFINS

1	11-ounce can mandarin oranges, drained and cut in half
1½	cups unsalted all-purpose flour
½	cup sugar
1¾	teaspoons baking powder
½	teaspoon ground nutmeg
½	teaspoon salt
¼	teaspoon allspice
⅓	cup butter, softened
½	cup milk
1	egg, beaten

Topping:

¼	cup sugar
½	teaspoon ground cinnamon
⅓	cup butter, melted

Preheat the oven to 350°. Line a muffin pan with paper baking cups. Drain the oranges and set aside. In a large mixing bowl combine the flour, sugar, baking powder, nutmeg, salt, and allspice. Cut in the butter to resemble coarse meal. Add the milk and egg and stir until the dry ingredients are moistened. Gently stir in the oranges. Fill the muffin cups three-fourths full. Bake for 20 to 25 minutes.

In a small bowl combine the sugar and cinnamon for topping. While hot, dip the tops of the muffins into melted butter, then roll in the sugar mixture.

Makes 2 dozen muffins.

Shirley Beattie
Presley-Ites Fan Club
Orlando, Florida

ELVIS BOUGHT THE CIRCLE G RANCH IN WALLS, MISSISSIPPI, IN FEBRUARY 1967, WHERE NASH AND EARL PRITCHETT LIVED FOR A FEW YEARS. THE COUPLE LATER MOVED TO A TRAILER ON GRACELAND.

★ STRANGER IN THE CROWD ★ STRAWBERRY FIG PRESERVES

½   cup water
3   cups peeled and mashed figs
3   cups sugar
2   3-ounce boxes strawberry or rasp-
     berry gelatin

In a saucepan bring the water to a boil. Place the figs in the boiling water and boil for about 2 minutes. In a bowl combine the sugar and gelatin and mix together. Add to the pot of boiling figs. Boil together for about 3 minutes. Pour into sterile jars and seal.
Makes 4 jars.

Kim Blackburn Poss
Cousin of Elvis Presley

★ GUITAR MAN GARLIC SAUCE FOR BREAD ★

½   cup (1 stick) butter
1   tablespoon minced garlic
1   tablespoon Italian seasoning
1   loaf Italian or French bread

Preheat the oven to 350°. In a saucepan melt the butter and add the garlic and Italian seasoning. Cook until bubbling. Remove from the heat and roll the bread in the sauce. Bake for 10 minutes.

Shane Sullivan and Mark Marascalco
Memphis, Tennessee

Main Dishes

★ FAMILY PLAIN CHEESE OMELETTE ★

Bacon drippings
2 eggs
1 tablespoon butter
Pinch salt
Pepper to taste
½ cup grated cheese

In a skillet or omelette pan, heat enough bacon drippings to thoroughly coat the inside of the pan. In a bowl whip the eggs, butter, salt, and pepper into a smooth consistency with a fork or wire whisk. Pour the egg mixture into the hot pan. When the omelette is cooked about halfway through, sprinkle the grated cheese completely over the omelette. Continue cooking until the cheese begins to melt and the egg is cooked. Fold the omelette closed and serve immediately.
Makes 1 omelette.

Hood/Presley family recipe

★ BIG BOWL OF OATMEAL ★

3 cups water
Dash salt
1½ cups old-fashioned Quaker oats
(not instant)
2 to 3 tablespoons butter
Milk
Sugar

Bring the water and salt to a boil in a saucepan. Add the oats, reduce the heat to medium, and cook for about 5 minutes. (Elvis liked his oatmeal to be really thick.) Stir in the butter. Place the oatmeal in a large bowl (or 2 or 3 smaller bowls). Add a little milk and sugar to taste.
Serves 1 to 3.

Edie Hand
Cousin of Elvis Presley

★ SUNSHINE BREAKFAST CASSEROLE ★

2	**slices loaf bread, cubed**
2	**pounds sausage, cooked, drained, and crumbled**
1	**cup grated sharp Cheddar cheese**
6	**eggs**
2	**cups milk**
2	**tablespoons dry mustard**
1	**teaspoon salt**

Preheat the oven to 375°. Lightly butter a 9 x 13-inch casserole dish. Spread the cubed bread in the bottom. Sprinkle the sausage over it, then pour the cheese on top. In a large bowl beat together the eggs, milk, dry mustard, and salt. Pour the egg mixture over the cheese. Bake for 45 minutes. This can be prepared the night before, covered, and refrigerated. Pop in the oven the next morning!

Serves 6.

Helen Benton
Tampa, Florida

Posing with their new Ford Fairlane in 1957 are Elvis's grandfather Jesse Presley and his second wife, Vera. (Elvis's twin brother, Jessie, was named after his grandfather.)

★ BIG CITY OMELETTE ★

2   **eggs**
    Pinch salt
    Fresh ground pepper
1   **tablespoon butter**

Suggested Fillings:
    Chopped Swiss or Cheddar cheese
    Cubed ham
    Sliced green peppers
    Chopped onions or scallions
    Crumbled cooked bacon

In a small bowl beat the eggs lightly with a fork, and add salt and pepper. Heat a skillet over medium heat and add the butter. When the butter is very hot, pour in the eggs and stir continuously—holding the fork flat until the eggs have set and holes appear in the mixture. Spread the eggs to cover the surface of the pan, and add filling to the side of the pan opposite the handle. Tilt the pan away from you and allow the unfilled half of the omelette to fall over the filled side. Cover with a plate and then invert the pan to remove the omelette.
    Serves 1.

Lucille Luongo
Elvis fan and Past National President,
American Women in Radio and Television
New York, New York

Elvis's Number 1 Hits

"Heartbreak Hotel"
"I Want You I Need You I Love You"
"Don't Be Cruel"
"Hound Dog"
"Love Me Tender"
"Too Much"
"All Shook Up/That's When Your Heartaches Begin"
"Let Me Be Your Teddy Bear"
"Jailhouse Rock"

"Don't"
"Hard Headed Woman"
"A Big Hunk O' Love"
"Stuck on You"
"It's Now or Never"
"Are You Lonesome Tonight"
"Surrender"
"Good Luck Charm"
"Suspicious Minds"

★ SENTIMENTAL ME ★
SAUSAGE BREAKFAST CASSEROLE

6   slices bread
     Enough butter or margarine to
        spread on bread
1   **pound bulk pork sausage**
1½   **cups shredded longhorn cheese**
6   **eggs, beaten**
2   **cups half and half**
     Salt to taste

Remove the crusts from the bread and spread butter or margarine on the slices. Place in a greased 9 x 13-inch baking dish and set aside.

In a skillet cook the sausage until browned, stirring to crumble. Drain well, and then spoon the sausage over the bread slices. Sprinkle cheese on top. In a separate bowl combine the eggs, half and half, and salt. Mix well and pour over the cheese. Cover the casserole and chill overnight.

Preheat the oven to 350°. Remove from the refrigerator 15 minutes before baking. Bake the casserole uncovered for 45 minutes or until set.

Serves 6.

Toni Drummond
Jasper, Alabama

ALL ABOARD—Elvis boards his jet to entertain fans at another destination.

★ CAN'T HELP FALLING IN LOVE ★ COUNTRY FRIED STEAK

Round Steak
Shortening

Wet Mix:
2 **eggs**
1 **cup milk**
Salt and pepper to taste

Dry Mix:
1 **cup all-purpose flour**
Salt and pepper to taste

Gravy:
1 **cup milk**
All-purpose flour
Salt and pepper

In a skillet melt the shortening, using enough to almost cover the steak pieces. In a separate bowl combine the eggs, milk, salt, and pepper. Dredge the round steak through the wet mixture. In a large plastic bag combine the flour with salt and pepper to taste. Drop the steak in the bag and shake until fully coated. Take the steak out of the bag and drop it into the hot skillet and cook until golden brown. Remove the steak and place it in an oven to keep warm.

Drain all of the oil from the pan except for 1 tablespoon. Keep all of the crisp bits in the skillet that fell to the bottom while cooking the meat. Pour in a cup of milk and bring to a boil. Sprinkle with flour until you get a creamy consistency. Do this slowly and stir constantly. Don't put in too much flour or it will get too stiff. If it is too stiff, add a little water and stir. Season with salt and pepper to taste.

Serves 6 to 8.

Ovaline Marchant
Vance, Alabama

WHEN ELVIS'S MOTHER GLADYS PRESLEY DIED, THE BLACKWOOD BROTHERS WERE ASKED TO SING AT HER FUNERAL. JAMES BLACKWOOD LATER RECOUNTED HOW ELVIS LEANED OVER HIS MOTHER'S CASKET AND SAID, "MAMA, I WOULD GIVE EVERY DIME I HAVE TO HAVE YOU BACK."

★ FRANKIE AND JOHNNY'S ★ COUNTRY FRIED STEAK

½ teaspoon salt
½ teaspoon pepper
1 ½ cups self-rising flour
1 cup oil
4 to 6 pieces of select cubed steak
1 medium onion, chopped
3 cups water

In a shallow pan or on a platter combine the salt, pepper, and flour. Flour the steak on both sides. Set the remaining flour aside. In a large skillet heat the oil over medium-high heat. Add the steak and brown on both sides. Remove the steak from the skillet. Reduce the heat, add the onion, and sauté until tender. In a small bowl combine the remaining flour and water. Blend well. Pour the flour mixture into the skillet and stir slowly until the gravy begins to thicken. Return the steaks to the skillet, turn over, and simmer over low heat for 15 to 20 minutes.
Serves 4 to 6.

Betty Jo McMichael
Co-owner, Whistle Stop Cafe
Irondale, Alabama

ELVIS CAME UP WITH HIS SLOGAN "TAKING CARE OF BUSINESS" TO SUM UP HIS WORK ETHIC. HE HAD GOLD NECKLACES DESIGNED WITH A LIGHTNING BOLT INSIGNIA. HE GAVE ONE TO EACH MEMBER OF THE MEMPHIS MAFIA AND TO FAMILY MEMBERS. THE WOMEN IN HIS LIFE GOT JEWELRY WITH THE INITIALS "TLC" (TENDER LOVING CARE).

★ BAREFOOT BALLAD BARBECUED SPARE RIBS ★

3	pounds spare ribs
¼	cup butter
½	cup chopped onion
1	clove garlic, minced
2	8-ounce cans tomato sauce
⅓	cup water
¼	cup steak seasoning sauce
2	tablespoons lemon
2	tablespoons white vinegar
2	teaspoons chili powder
2	teaspoons salt
4	dashes steak seasoning sauce

Preheat the oven to 350°. Put the ribs in a shallow roasting pan and roast uncovered for 1 hour and 30 minutes. Pour off the fat. Set aside while making the sauce.

In a saucepan melt the butter and sauté the onion and garlic. Add the remaining ingredients and bring to a boil. Pour the sauce over the ribs. Return the ribs to the oven and roast, basting frequently, for 30 minutes.

Serves 6 to 8.

Marjorie Bonfils
Washington, D.C.

Cousins Donna Presley Early and Edie Hand enjoy looking through a family scrapbook.

★ BURNING LOVE BARBECUE SAUCE ★

1	**3½-quart bottle ketchup**
½	**gallon white vinegar**
2	**cups water**
½	**cup sugar**
2	**tablespoons salt**
2	**tablespoons black pepper**
½	**tablespoon cayenne pepper**
2½	**tablespoons barbecue spice**
	Juice of 1 lemon

In a large stock pot mix all of the ingredients and bring to a boil over high heat. Stir well.

Reduce the heat and simmer for 1 hour and 30 minutes, stirring often. Let the sauce cool. Pour the sauce into sterilized jars and tighten the lids. Store in the refrigerator. It will keep for several weeks.

Makes about 6 quarts.

Bill McMichael
Co-owner, Whistle Stop Cafe
Irondale, Alabama

Match the Plot with the Title of the Elvis Movie (Part One)

1.	*Blue Hawaii*	A.	American soldier stationed in Germany bets pals he can win heart of nightclub singer
2.	*Charro!*	B.	Movie star is kidnapped in the Middle East
3.	*Double Trouble*	C.	Convicted killer is released from prison to become moody recording artist
4.	*Follow That Dream*	D.	Young Southern farmer marries his older brother's sweetheart
5.	*Fun in Acapulco*	E.	Stock car driver meets beautiful tax inspector
6.	*G.I. Blues*	F.	Carnie becomes singing star
7.	*Harum Scarum*	G.	Social worker encourages backwoods youth to live up to potential as writer
8.	*It Happened at the World's Fair*	H.	Race car driver enters the Grand Prix
9.	*Jailhouse Rock*	I.	Son of a rich family becomes tour guide to group from all-girl school
10.	*Live a Little, Love a Little*	J.	Unemployed pilot escorts young girl for a day at fair and falls for nurse
11.	*Love Me Tender*	K.	Backwoods singer and his father look after orphans while homesteading on government land
12.	*Roustabout*	L.	Magazine photographer shoots beautiful girls for conservative magazine and "girlie" mag
13.	*Speedway*	M.	Touring Chautauqua company disrupts life in small town
14.	*Trouble With Girls*	N.	An outlaw turns good but is framed by his old gang
15.	*Viva Las Vegas*	O.	Acrobatic lifeguard confronts his fear of heights
16.	*Wild in the Country*	P.	Singer breezes through Europe with heiress and jewel thieves

ANSWERS: 1. I, 2. N, 3. P, 4. K, 5. O, 6. A, 7. B, 8. J, 9. C, 10. L, 11. D, 12. F, 13. E, 14. M, 15. H, 16. G

★ Dr. Judy's Fried Spare Ribs ★

4 **pounds spare ribs**
1 **clove garlic**
 Salt and pepper
 Water

Spare Rib Gravy:
2 **tablespoons all-purpose flour**
3 **tablespoons cream**
½ **cup milk**

Ask the butcher to cut the spare ribs in half, horizontally. At home, cut the ribs into uniform-sized chunks. Rub the garlic clove around the bottom and sides of a large, heavy kettle with a tight-fitting lid. Put the ribs in the kettle and add enough cold water to come up to the level of the meat. Season with about 1 teaspoon each of salt and pepper. Cover tightly and cook over high heat until the water boils. Reduce the heat to medium and let the ribs cook until all of the water evaporates (this takes several hours). When you begin to hear the meat sizzle reduce the heat, remove the kettle lid, and let the ribs fry crisp in their own fat. Turn them occasionally so they're brown on both sides.

Remove the ribs from the kettle and pour off all of the fat except ½ cup. Sprinkle the flour into the remaining fat. Turn up the heat and stir the flour around in the fat until richly browned. Remove from the stove and blend in the cream and milk. Return to the stove and stir until smooth and bubbly over low heat. If the gravy is too thick for your taste, stir in enough hot water to make it just right.
 Serves 6 to 8.

Dr. Judy Kuriansky

Talk show host and author Dr. Judy Kuriansky (right, during a lecture with Edie Hand) once said, "As a psychologist, I know you only fully know a person when you know and understand his family and roots....To know Elvis's sensitive, smart, and spiritual relatives is to cherish and adore them, and the man they loved, supported, and tried to protect."

★ ROUSTABOUT CHUCK ROAST ★

3   pounds chuck roast
1   cup all-purpose flour
1   10¾-ounce can golden mushroom
    soup
1   6-ounce package dry onion soup
    mix
2   soup cans water
    Sliced potatoes, optional
    Sliced onions, optional
    Sliced carrots, optional

Preheat the oven to 350°. Rub the flour over the chuck roast. In a cast-iron skillet brown the meat over medium heat. Add the remaining ingredients, and then bake for 1 hour and 30 minutes to 2 hours. You may add potatoes, onions, and carrots during the last 30 minutes of cooking.

Serves 6.

Kim Blackburn Poss
Cousin of Elvis Presley

Kim Poss (left) and sister Edie Hand hug at a Christmas parade near Tupelo, Mississippi, in 1992.

★ BRITCHES BARBECUE BRISKET ★

2	teaspoons barbecue sauce
2	teaspoons steak seasoning sauce
1	teaspoon garlic salt
1	teaspoon onion salt
2	teaspoons celery seed
1½	teaspoons salt
1	teaspoon pepper
1	3- to 4-pound brisket

Sauce:

1	cup ketchup
¾	cup water
1½	tablespoons firmly packed brown sugar
3	tablespoons steak seasoning sauce
4	tablespoons vinegar
1½	teaspoons sugar
¼	cup chopped onion

In a bowl combine the barbecue sauce, 2 teaspoons steak seasoning sauce, garlic salt, onion salt, celery seed, salt, and pepper. Rub both sides of the meat with the seasoning mixture. Cover the pan with foil and refrigerate overnight. Preheat the oven to 300°. Bake for 3 hours.

In a saucepan blend the ketchup, water, brown sugar, 3 tablespoons of steak seasoning sauce, vinegar, sugar, and onion. Bring to a boil and let boil for 10 minutes.

During the last hour of cooking, brush the sauce on the brisket. Let the meat stand for a few minutes before carving.

Serves 6 to 8.

Verna Melohn
Elvis fan

★ SOLDIER BOY SALISBURY STEAK ★

2	pounds extra-lean ground beef chuck
1½	cups finely chopped onion
2	eggs
2	tablespoons steak seasoning sauce
1	teaspoon seasoned salt
1	teaspoon pepper
1	teaspoon garlic salt
1	cup sifted self-rising flour
½	cup oil
1½	to 2 cups water

In a large bowl combine the chuck, onion, eggs, steak seasoning sauce, seasoned salt, pepper, and garlic salt, and mix well. Shape the mixture into 8 balls, pressing to ½-inch thickness. Flour both sides. In a skillet heat the oil. Reduce the heat to medium high. Add the meat patties and brown on both sides, cooking for about 10 minutes. Remove the patties from the pan and set aside.

Mix the remaining flour with the water and blend well. Add the flour mixture to the skillet and stir until the gravy thickens. Return the patties to the pan and reduce the heat and simmer for 10 to 15 minutes.

Serves 4.

Betty Jo McMichael
Co-owner, Whistle Stop Cafe
Irondale, Alabama

★ ELVIS'S FAVORITE ROAST BEEF ★

Beef roast

In a skillet brown the meat on both sides and marinate with seasoning salt. Sprinkle a little garlic onto the meat. Wrap the meat in aluminum foil and place in a 350° oven for 2 hours.

Mary Jenkins
Personal cook for Elvis Presley

Mary Jenkins in the kitchen at Graceland, where she cooked for Elvis and family for many years.

★ MOODY BLUE MEAT LOAF ★

1 **pound hamburger meat**
½ **cup regular oats**
1½ **teaspoons salt**
1 **egg**
⅔ **cup tomato juice or canned tomatoes**
1 **medium onion, chopped**

Preheat the oven to 350°. In a large bowl mix all of the ingredients together. Place the meat in a loaf pan and cook for 45 minutes or until cooked to the desired doneness.

Serves 6.

Kim Blackburn Poss
Cousin of Elvis Presley

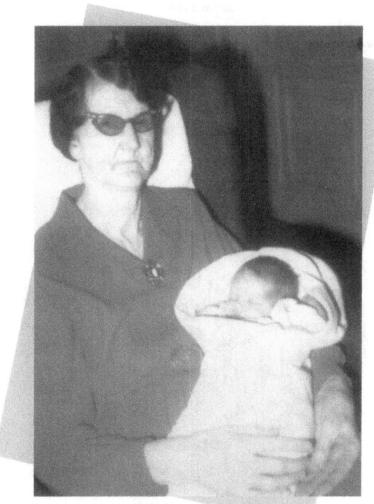

Elvis's grandmother Dodger holds her newborn great-granddaughter Lisa Marie.

★ Mom's Memphis Meat Loaf ★

2	tablespoons margarine
¼	cup minced onion
1	rib celery, chopped
½	green pepper, minced
2½	pounds ground chuck
½	cup quick-cooking oats
½	cup bottled cocktail sauce
2	eggs, beaten
¾	teaspoon salt
1	teaspoon thyme
1	teaspoon black pepper
2	cups shredded low-fat Cheddar cheese

Preheat the oven to 350°. In a skillet melt the margarine and sauté the onion, celery, and green pepper over low heat for 10 to 15 minutes or until tender. In a large mixing bowl combine the sautéed vegetables and the remaining ingredients and blend well. Spray a bread loaf pan with cooking spray. Place the mixture in the pan and smooth the top. Bake for 1 hour or until well browned.

Let stand for about 5 minutes, then carefully remove the loaf from the pan. Drain on brown paper and let stand for 10 minutes before slicing.

Serves 5 to 6.

Jill McQuown
Memphis, Tennessee

Dodger Presley (left) and son Vernon pose with their landlady in the neighborhood around the home they shared with Elvis while he was stationed at Bad Nauheim, Germany.

★ MYSTERY TRAIN MEAT LOAF ★

2   slices white bread, no crusts
½   cup milk
2   pounds meat loaf mix (beef, veal,
    and pork)
1   medium onion, minced
1   tablespoon steak seasoning sauce
½   cup ketchup
½   teaspoon salt
½   teaspoon pepper
2   eggs
2   tablespoons firmly packed brown
    sugar

Glaze:
1   tablespoon sugar
1   tablespoon mustard

Preheat the oven to 375°. In a bowl soak the bread in the milk for a few minutes. In a large bowl combine the meat, soaked breadcrumbs, onion, steak seasoning sauce, ketchup, salt, pepper, eggs, and brown sugar and stir until well blended. Put the mixture into a well-greased loaf pan. Bake for 45 minutes.

In a small bowl combine the sugar and mustard and brush over the meat loaf and cook for 15 minutes more.

Serves 6 to 8.

Edie Hand
Cousin of Elvis Presley

ELVIS DIDN'T DINE AT MEMPHIS RESTAURANTS VERY OFTEN. HE WOULD PHONE IN ORDERS AND HAVE MEALS DELIVERED BECAUSE HE WOULD HAVE BEEN MOBBED IF HE HAD EATEN IN PUBLIC. AMONG HIS FAVORITE PLACES IN THE CITY ON THE BLUFFS OF THE MISSISSIPPI WERE THE RENDEZVOUS WITH ITS RIBS AND BARBECUE AND A MEXICAN EATERY CALLED PANCHO'S. AS FOR FAST FOODS, HE LOVED WHATTABURGER'S HAMBURGERS.

★ HARUM SCARUM BARBECUED HAMBURGERS ★

1½ to 2 pounds lean ground chuck
1 cup quick oats
1 small onion, chopped
  Pinch salt
  Pinch pepper
  Pinch garlic powder
1 12-ounce can evaporated milk
1 15-ounce bottle barbecue sauce

In a large bowl mix the meat, oats, onion, salt, pepper, and garlic powder. Add the milk and stir well. Shape the meat into patties. In a skillet brown the patties on both sides. Cover with your favorite barbecue sauce and let simmer for 45 minutes. You may have to add a little water while it cooks. This can be made in advance, left in the sauce, and reheated later.
Serves 6.

Linc Hand
Cousin of Elvis Presley

Dodger Presley inside the home where she stayed with Elvis during his tour of duty in Germany.

★ PALM BEACH BURGER ★

1 **hamburger patty**
1 **hamburger bun**
1 **tablespoon pimiento cheese**
  Mayonnaise
  Crisp lettuce
  Pickle rings

Elvis's favorite hamburger.

Place the hamburger patty and bun on the grill. After cooking the hamburger on one side, turn it over and cook it on the other side. While the second side is cooking, spread the pimiento cheese on the bun top and place it on the cooked side of the hamburger. While the hamburger continues to cook, spread mayonnaise on the bottom bun and then place a piece of lettuce and some pickle rings on top. When the hamburger is cooked, place it on the bottom bun and serve.
    Serves 1.

The Gridiron Restaurant
Memphis, Tennessee

Vester Presley stands proudly beside the new car given to him by his nephew Elvis in 1970.

★ You Ain't Nothin' But a Hot Dog ★

1   **pound ground beef, browned and drained**
2   **small cans tomato sauce**
2   **6-ounce cans tomato paste**
2   **onions, diced**
2   **tablespoons oil**
1   **tablespoon chili powder**
2   **cups water**
¼   **cup garlic powder**
      Cumin to taste
      Salt to taste
      Foot-long hot dogs

In a large pot combine the ground beef, tomato sauce, tomato paste, onions, oil, chili powder, water, garlic powder, cumin, and salt. Simmer for 10 minutes.

Pour the mixture over foot-long hot dogs and serve.

Carlene Sowards
Memphis, Tennessee

An early photograph of Elvis's aunt Delta Presley Biggs.

★ BEYOND THE BEND BEEFY BREAD ROLL ★

1	pound hamburger or sausage
1	small onion, chopped
1	cup sweet relish
½	green bell pepper, chopped
1	egg, beaten
2	cups (8 ounces) shredded cheese (Cheddar works well)
4	to 5 tablespoons barbecue sauce
1	loaf frozen bread dough

In a skillet brown the meat with the onion, relish, and green pepper. Drain the grease and add the egg, cheese, and barbecue sauce.

Preheat the oven to 350°. Roll the bread dough out until it is thin. Pour a large spoonful of beef mixture along the width of the bread. Roll the bread one turn, pour another spoonful of beef mixture along the width, roll one turn, pour on more of the beef mix, turn, and continue until all of the mixture is gone.

Bake for 25 minutes.

Serves 6.

Shirley Beattie
Presley-Ites Fan Club
Orlando, Florida

Photo by David McGough

Elvis's aunt Delta poses with Edmund I, a Pomeranian shared by Delta and Elvis, and palomino Rising Sun, Elvis's favorite horse.

★ CHARRO CHEESEBURGER PIE ★

1   **cup tomato sauce**
½   **cup diced onion**
½   **medium green bell pepper, diced**
1   **3-ounce packet instant beef broth and seasoning mix**
     Artificial sweetener equaling 1 teaspoon sugar
½   **teaspoon chili powder**
¼   **teaspoon garlic powder**
8   **ounces cooked ground beef, crumbled**
1   **cup (4 ounces) grated Cheddar cheese**
2   **cups cooked enriched rice**

Preheat the oven to 375°. In a medium saucepan combine the tomato sauce, onion, bell pepper, beef broth mix, sweetener, chili powder, and garlic powder. Simmer for 8 to 10 minutes or until the vegetables are tender.

Add the beef, ¾ cup of cheese, and the rice. Stir until the cheese melts. Turn the mixture into a greased 8-inch square baking dish. Sprinkle with the remaining cheese, and bake for 30 minutes.

Allow the pie to sit for 10 to15 minutes before cutting. Divide evenly.

Serves 4.

Georgann Reynolds
In Memory of Mabel Busby
Elvis Country Fan Club

Elvis's first cousins, sisters Susie and Donna Pritchett, giggle for the camera while standing behind a friend's red Chrysler while visiting Graceland in about 1959.

★ UNCHAINED MELODY BEEFY MEXICAN ★ CORN BREAD

Cornmeal Mix:

1 cup cornmeal
¼ teaspoon salt
1 cup milk
1 16-ounce can creamed corn
½ teaspoon baking soda
2 eggs

Beef Filling:

1 pound ground meat
3 jalapeños
2 cups (8 ounces) grated cheese
1 large onion, finely chopped

In a large bowl combine the cornmeal, salt, milk, corn, baking soda, and eggs. Mix well and set aside.

Preheat the oven to 300°. In a skillet brown the meat. Drain off the excess fat. Add the cheese, onion, and jalapeños to the browned meat and stir to mix all together. Grease a 9 x 13-inch pan and pour half of the cornmeal mixture into the pan. Spread the meat mixture into the pan and top with the other half of the cornmeal mix. Bake for 1 hour.

Serves 6.

Marva Kaye Ward
Elvis Country Fan Club

Two-year-old Jamie Early with his grandfather Earl Pritchett and mother, Donna Presley Early in front of Graceland in 1978.

★ Beginner's Luck Barbecue Bean Bake ★

1	pound ground beef
1	pound bacon
1	medium onion, chopped
½	cup ketchup
½	cup barbecue sauce
1	teaspoon salt
¼	cup prepared mustard
¼	cup molasses
1	teaspoon chili powder
¾	teaspoon pepper
2	16-ounce cans red kidney beans
2	16-ounce cans pork and beans
2	16-ounce cans butter beans

Preheat the oven to 350°. In a large skillet brown the beef, bacon, and onion. Drain. In a large bowl combine the browned meat, ketchup, barbecue sauce, salt, mustard, molasses, chili powder, and pepper. Stir well. Then add the beans and mix well. Transfer to a large casserole dish. Bake for 1 hour.

Serves 4 to 6.

Carlene Sowards
Memphis, Tennessee

★ Spinout Spaghetti ★

1	16-ounce package spaghetti
1	pound lean ground beef
12	ounces sliced mushrooms
8	ounces ketchup
2	20-ounce jars spaghetti sauce with vegetables
	Salt and pepper to taste

Cook the spaghetti until soft in a large pot of boiling water. In a large pot, completely brown the meat and drain. Add the mushrooms and simmer until browned. Then add the sauces and salt and pepper to taste. Simmer until hot and then add the cooked spaghetti.

Giano Fioni
Palermo, Italy

★ BEN'S SPAGHETTI AND MEAT SAUCE ★

2   **tablespoons butter**
½   **medium onion, chopped**
1½   **pounds ground round**
     Italian seasoning
     Salt and pepper to taste
     Garlic salt to taste
1   **to 2 16-ounce cans tomato sauce**
1   **16-ounce can tomato juice**

In a skillet melt the butter and sauté the onion. Add the ground round and cook until the meat is well done. Drain the fat off the meat and add the Italian seasoning, salt, pepper, and garlic salt to taste. Add the tomato sauce and can of tomato juice (you can throw in another can of tomato juice, depending on how thick you like your sauce). Cover and simmer for 15 to 30 minutes. Serve over spaghetti, angel hair, or your choice of pasta.

Serves 4 to 6.

Ben Speer
The Speer Family
Ben Speer sang with Elvis.
He sang backup for Elvis on "I Want You, I Need You, I Love You."
He is also the publisher of Elvis's gospel hit
"When I Walk 'Dem Golden Stairs."

Ben Speer and Edie Hand reminisce at Mel's Diner in Pigeon Forge, Tennessee, about Ben's singing backup on Elvis's recording "I Want You, I Need You, I Love You." Also singing backup on that 1950s recording were Ben's brother, Brock, and Gordon Stoker.

★ LAWDY MISS CLAWDY LASAGNA ★

1	pound ground meat
1	medium onion, chopped (about 1 cup)
1	clove garlic, crushed
2	tablespoons parsley flakes
1	teaspoon dried basil leaves
½	teaspoon salt
1	teaspoon sugar
1	16-ounce can whole tomatoes, undrained
1	15-ounce tomato sauce
12	uncooked lasagna noodles
1	16-ounce carton ricotta cheese (or 2-cups creamed cottage cheese)
½	cup grated Parmesan cheese
1	tablespoon parsley flakes
1½	teaspoons dried oregano leaves
2	cups shredded mozzarella cheese

In a 10-inch skillet cook and stir the ground meat, onion, and garlic until the meat is browned. Drain and stir in the parsley flakes, basil, salt, sugar, tomatoes, and tomato sauce. Break up the tomatoes. Heat to boiling, stirring occasionally. Reduce the heat and simmer uncovered until slightly thickened (about 45 minutes).

Cook the noodles as directed on the package; drain. In a bowl mix together the ricotta cheese, Parmesan cheese, parsley, and oregano.

Preheat the oven to 350°. Spread 1 cup of sauce mixture in an ungreased 9 x 13-inch baking dish. Top with 4 noodles. Spread 1 cup of the cheese mixture over the noodles. Spread 1 cup of the sauce mixture on top. Sprinkle with ⅔ cup of the mozzarella cheese. Top with the remaining noodles and sauce mixture. Sprinkle with the remaining mozzarella cheese and Parmesan cheese. Bake about 45 minutes uncovered until hot and bubbly.

Let stand for about 15 minutes before cutting.
Serves 8.

Marlene Nunez
Elvis Country Fan Club

Elvis's Uncle Earl Pritchett proudly stands in front of Graceland with daughters Susie (left) and Donna in this 1978 photo. They lived in a mobile home on property behind Graceland for several years.

★ LOVING ARMS VEGETARIAN LASAGNA ★

1   16-ounce carton light ricotta cheese
1   egg
1   cup chopped medium onions
2   cloves garlic
2   tablespoons olive oil
½   cup chopped celery
½   cup chopped green pepper
1   tablespoon sugar
1   15-ounce can tomatoes
1   8-ounce can tomato paste
    Oregano
1   bunch parsley, chopped
    Precooked lasagna noodles
4   cups (1 pound) grated or sliced
        grated mozzarella
½   cup grated Parmesan cheese
1   pound fresh spinach, cleaned and
        chopped
1   cup chopped fresh tomatoes
    Basil
    Thyme

In a medium bowl mix the ricotta and egg together for easier spreading. Make the tomato mixture by sautéing the onions and garlic in the olive oil. Then add the celery, pepper, sugar, canned tomatoes, tomato paste, some oregano, and chopped parsley. Let simmer for 1 hour, stirring as needed.

Preheat the oven to 350°. In a large pan layer the tomato mixture, lasagna noodles, ricotta, mozzarella, some Parmesan, and then the chopped spinach and tomatoes. Put the sauce on top. Sprinkle Parmesan on top. Bake for 1 hour.

Let stand for 10 minutes for better cutting and serving. Sprinkle the chopped fresh tomatoes on the very top. Sprinkle lightly with oregano, basil, and thyme, and then sprinkle Parmesan over all.

Serves 8.

Judith Murray
Toronto, Ontario

★ Pledging My Love Vegetable Pizza ★

2   **packages refrigerator crescent dinner rolls**

2   **8-ounce packages cream cheese, softened**

1   **1-ounce package dry ranch dressing mix**

¼   **cup chopped celery**

½   **cup chopped onions**

¼   **cup cauliflower, chopped into florets**

⅛   **cup chopped radishes**

½   **cup chopped lettuce**

½   **cup chopped tomatoes**

½   **cup chopped broccoli**

½   **cup chopped carrots**

Piece together the crescent rolls to form a pizza crust. Bake according to the package directions.

In a medium bowl mix together the cream cheese with the dry ranch mix. Spread over the baked crust. Top with the chopped vegetables.

Serves 4.

Verna Melohn
Elvis fan

Elvis's first cousin Donna in 1968, the year she graduated from high school.

★ COLETTA'S BARBECUE PIZZA ★

Dough:

1   ¼-ounce package dry yeast
1   cup warm water
3½ cups all-purpose flour
1   teaspoon salt
¼   cup olive oil

Sauce:

1   cup ketchup
½   cup tomato paste
½   cup tomato purée
1   teaspoon white vinegar
1   tablespoon Worcestershire sauce
3   whole cloves
½   cup sliced onions
⅛   teaspoon garlic powder
2   teaspoons sugar
½   teaspoon salt
½   teaspoon black pepper
1   teaspoon dried basil
¾   cup water

2   cups barbecue sauce
12 ounces reduced-fat mozzarella
      cheese, shredded
2   ounces processed cheese, shredded
1¾ pounds barbecued pork shoulder,
      chopped and heated

This was Elvis's favorite pizza.

Dissolve the yeast in ¼ cup of the warm water and set aside. Combine the flour and salt in a mixing bowl. Make a well in the center of the flour. Add the yeast mixture, the oil, and remaining ¾ cup of water. Mix with a wooden spoon until a ball of dough forms and the dough cleans the side of the bowl. Turn the dough out of the bowl onto a lightly floured surface. Knead the dough for 7 to 8 minutes until it is smooth and like satin. (Dust the dough with flour if it's too sticky.) Lightly dust a large mixing bowl with flour. Place the dough in the bowl and cover with plastic wrap and a towel. Allow the dough to rise in a warm place for about 90 minutes, or until it doubles in bulk.

After the dough rises, punch it down and turn it out of the bowl onto a lightly floured surface. Knead gently for about 2 minutes. Roll or stretch the dough into a circle that is 16 inches in diameter and about ¼-inch thick. Place the dough in a 16-inch flat pizza pan. Cover the dough with a clean towel and let it rise a second time for about 45 minutes before adding the toppings.

Combine all of the sauce ingredients in a 2-quart saucepan and bring to a boil. Reduce the heat and simmer for 20 minutes, stirring frequently. Remove the pan from the heat and strain to remove the cloves and onion. Let the sauce cool to room temperature. (The sauce can be made a day or 2 day ahead of time.) Yields 2 cups of strained sauce.

To make the pizza, preheat the oven to 500°. Spread ⅔ cup of the barbecue sauce evenly over the dough to within ½ inch of the edge. Mix the shredded cheeses and spread over the sauce. Bake the pizza in the hot oven for about 10 minutes or until the crust is golden brown and the cheese is bubbly. Remove the pizza from the oven and spread the barbecued meat over the cheese. Heat the remaining barbecue sauce and pour evenly over the pizza. Serve immediately.

Makes 1 16-inch pizza.

Coletta's Italian Restaurant
Memphis, Tennessee

★ PUPPET ON A STRING COUNTRY FRIED PORK ★

12	**thin pork chops**
	Salt and pepper to taste
1	**large onion, diced**
3	**tablespoons butter**
3	**tablespoons all-purpose flour**
2	**cups milk**
1	**teaspoon Worcestershire sauce**
	Salt and pepper to taste

Place the pork chops in a cold heavy skillet and cook over medium heat, turning constantly so they brown evenly. Pour off the fat as it melts. When the chops are almost cooked, sprinkle generously with salt and pepper. (It should take about 15 minutes to brown the chops.) Place the chops in an uncovered dish and keep in a warming oven. Keep ¼ cup of fat in the skillet.

In the same skillet cook the onion until tender but not brown. While the onion is cooking, make a cream sauce.

In a saucepan melt the butter. Stir in the flour, and gradually add the milk. Cook over medium heat for 5 minutes. Add the cream sauce to the onions and heat. Stirring constantly, add the Worcestershire sauce and salt and pepper to taste. Put the chops on a serving dish and pour the cream sauce over them.

Serves 6.

Jennifer Mitchell
Cobourg, Ontario

THE PRESLEYS MIGRATED FROM TUPELO TO MEMPHIS IN 1948, WHERE THE FAMILY JOINED THE FIRST ASSEMBLY OF GOD CHURCH, WHERE ELVIS DEVELOPED HIS LOVE OF GOSPEL MUSIC. AUNT NASH WOULD LATER BECOME AN ASSEMBLIES OF GOD MINISTER. WHEN THAT HAPPENED, ELVIS PRESENTED HER WITH A GOLD PIANO FOR HER CHURCH. IT WAS A 1928 GOLD KIMBALL GRAND PIANO. THE PIANO WAS TOO LARGE FOR THE CHURCH BUILDING, SO SHE ASKED ELVIS IF SHE COULD TRADE IT IN. HE SAID YES, AND NASH'S HUSBAND, EARL, PULLED THE TRACTOR UP TO THE FRONT OF THE HOUSE AND MOVED THE PIANO OUT ON THE DIP OF THE TRACTOR. THE PIANO IS NOW OWNED BY THE 148 INVESTMENT GROUP OF AKRON, OHIO, AND IS ON DISPLAY AT THE COUNTRY MUSIC HALL OF FAME IN NASHVILLE. AUNT NASH ENDED UP GETTING A PINE WURLITZER.

★ FLIP-FLOP CHICKEN FRIED PORK CHOPS ★

6	pork chops, about ¾-inch thickness
2	eggs, beaten
2	tablespoons milk
1	cup fine cracker crumbs
¼	cup fat
½	teaspoon salt
	Dash pepper
¼	cup water

Pound the chops thoroughly with a meat pounder to ½ inch thickness. In a medium bowl mix the eggs and milk. Dip the chops first into the egg mixture, then into the crumbs. In a skillet heat the fat and brown the chops on both sides. Season with salt and pepper. Add water, cover, and cook over low heat for 45 to 60 minutes. Lift the chops occasionally to prevent sticking. For a crisp coating, remove the cover for the last 15 minutes.

Serves 6.

Edie Hand
Cousin of Elvis Presley

Elvis's aunt Nash Presley Pritchett preaches to her Assemblies of God congregation in Walls, Mississippi.

★ FAMILY FAVORITE FRIED PORK CHOPS ★

6	medium pork chops
1	teaspoon pepper
1	teaspoon salt
1½	cups flour
½	teaspoon paprika
½	teaspoon parsley flakes
⅓	cup vegetable oil

Wash the pork chops and pat dry. Sprinkle with salt and pepper. Let the pork chops stand for 5 minutes. Coat in a mixture of flour, paprika, and parsley flakes. Heat the oil in a skillet, place the pork chops in the skillet, and fry until golden brown.

Serves 3 to 6.

Presley/Hood Family Recipe

Minnie Mae "Dodger" Presley's grave immediately following her burial at Graceland in 1980.

★ PORK CHOPS SOFTLY AND TENDERLY ★

3	tablespoons butter
6	pork chops
1	teaspoon salt
⅛	teaspoon pepper
1½	cups buttermilk
½	bay leaf
2	tablespoons all-purpose flour
¼	cup water

In a skillet melt the butter and brown the chops on both sides. Add the seasonings, buttermilk, and bay leaf. Simmer for about 1 hour.

In a small bowl blend the water with flour to form a smooth paste. Remove the chops and stir the paste into pan. Cook until thickened. Serve the chops with the gravy.

Serves 6.

Linda Sue Hacker Whitaker
Cousin of Elvis Presley

DODGER GOT HER NICKNAME BECAUSE WHEN ELVIS WAS A YOUNG BOY HE COULDN'T PRO-NOUNCE GRANDMOTHER. HE COULD ONLY SAY "GRANDDODGER." OVER THE YEARS, HE JUST SHORTENED IT TO "DODGER." ONLY HE AND A CHOSEN FEW WERE ABLE TO CALL MINNIE MAE BY THAT NICKNAME.

★ PROMISED LAND PORK CHOPS AND GRAVY ★

½ cup all-purpose flour
1½ teaspoons dry mustard
½ teaspoon salt
½ teaspoon garlic powder
6 1-inch-thick, lean pork chops
1 10¾-ounce can chicken broth, undiluted
2 tablespoons vegetable oil

In a shallow dish combine the flour, dry mustard, salt, and garlic powder. Dredge the chops in the flour mixture and set aside. In a 3½-quart slow cooker or crock pot combine the remaining flour mixture and the chicken broth. Pour the oil into a large skillet and place over medium high heat until hot. Brown the chops in the hot oil on both sides, and then place the chops in the crock pot. Cover and cook on high for 2 hours and 30 minutes or until tender. Serve hot with rice or mashed potatoes.

Serves 6.

Cecil Blackwood
The Blackwood Brothers

One of Elvis's favorite gospel groups was the Blackwood Brothers. Pictured here (clockwise from top left) are Tommy Fairchild, Ken Turner, Jimmy Blackwood, Pat Hoffmaster, James Blackwood, and Cecil Blackwood.

★ AUNT ALICE'S GREAT PORK CHOP ★ SKILLET DINNER

6	lean pork chops
½	teaspoon salt
¼	teaspoon pepper
1	tablespoon cooking oil
½	teaspoon savory bay leaves
½	bay leaf
2	cups tomato juice
½	cup water
1	small cabbage, cut into 6 wedges
6	carrots, cut into one-inch pieces (about 2 cups)
1½	cups coarsely chopped onion
3	medium potatoes, pared and quartered
¼	teaspoon salt

Season the chops with the salt and pepper. In a large skillet heat the oil and brown the chops. Add the bay leaves, tomato juice, and water. Cover and simmer for 30 minutes. Add the cabbage, carrots, onion, potatoes, and salt. Cover and simmer for 35 minutes or until the vegetables are tender.

Serves 6.

Alice Hood Hacker
Niece of Elvis Presley's grandmother Minnie Mae Hood Presley

Edie Hand and Donna Presley Early visit with Elvis's uncle Vester.

★ SCRATCH MY BACK SKEWERED PORK CHOPS ★

¼   cup lard (or as needed)

6   pork loin chops, about ¾-inch thick-
      ness

¼   cup (½ stick) butter

1   cup chopped onion

1   cup chopped celery

4   cups cubed day-old bread

1   teaspoon salt

½   teaspoon pepper

¼   cup chopped parsley

Preheat the oven to 325°. In a skillet heat a small amount of fat and brown the chops lightly. In a separate pan melt the butter and cook the onion and celery until golden but not brown.

In a medium bowl combine the bread, salt, pepper, and parsley. Add the onion and celery. Place a chop fat side up at each end of a 5 x 9-inch loaf pan. Alternate the chops and stuffing. Run skewers through the chops. Bake for 1 hour or until done.

Serves 6.

Varnice Hacker Humphries
Cousin of Elvis Presley

ELVIS ACTUALLY HAD LIGHT BROWN HAIR,
BUT HE THOUGHT HE LOOKED BETTER WITH
DARK HAIR, SO HE DYED IT.

★ HAVE A HAPPY DRIZZLED HAM BAKE ★

1½ **pounds ham, ground**
1½ **pounds fresh pork, ground**
1½ **cups breadcrumbs**
2   **eggs**
1¼ **cups milk**
1   **cup firmly packed brown sugar**
1   **tablespoon prepared mustard**
¼   **cup cider vinegar**
¼   **cup water**

Preheat the oven to 350°. In a large mixing bowl combine the ham, pork, breadcrumbs, eggs, and milk. Form the mixture into a loaf and place in a 5 x 9-inch loaf pan. Bake for 45 minutes.

In a saucepan combine the brown sugar, mustard, vinegar, and water. Boil the sauce ingredients for 5 minutes or until thick. Pour over the loaf and bake for an additional 45 minutes or longer.

Serves 6.

Charlotte Hacker Myrick
Cousin of Elvis Presley

*A blond Elvis at age 13 poses for this portrait
with his beloved mother, Gladys.*

★ BEACH BOY BLUES BEER BAKED HAM ★

1	**ham**
1	**jar whole cloves**
2	**12-ounce bottles beer**

Cut the ham with diagonal cuts, crisscrossing the fat side of the ham. Push the whole cloves into the cuts. Put the ham fat side up into a pan. Pour the beer over the ham. Bake according to the ham instructions. Baste often with the beer during baking.
Serves 6 to 8.

Phyllis Hopkins
Orlando, Florida
Elvis Presley Continentals of Florida

Nash Presley Pritchett is pleased with a
Parisian scarf given to her by a fan.

★ SMORGASBORD SMOTHERED HAM ★

1   **14-pound fully cooked ham, bone in**
½   **cup currant jelly**
2   **tablespoons prepared mustard**
¼   **cup firmly packed light brown sugar**
3   **cups finely rolled salted cracker crumbs**
6   **tablespoons butter, melted**

Preheat the oven to 325°. Place the ham fat side up on a rack. Place the rack in a shallow pan. Bake for 2 hours, allowing 10 to 15 minutes per pound or until a meat thermometer inserted in the ham reaches 130°.

Remove the ham from the oven, remove the rind, and turn the ham over. Increase the oven temperature to 425°.

In a saucepan heat the jelly, mustard, and sugar, stirring until smooth. Spread over the ham. Combine the cracker crumbs and butter. Pat evenly onto the ham. Return to the oven and bake for 15 minutes or until the crust is lightly browned.

Serves 10 to 12.

Adam Taylor
Co-Producer, "Elvis in Hollywood" documentary

Nash Presley Pritchett speaks to a convention of Elvis fans at the Presley family's Circle G Ranch in Mississippi.

★ PARTY CHICKEN ★

4	**boned chicken breasts**
1	**pound bacon**
8	**ounces sour cream**
1	**10¾-ounce can cream of mushroom soup**
	Pinch pepper

Preheat the oven to 300°. Roll the chicken breasts and place 1 or 2 strips of bacon over each one. Place the breasts in a casserole dish. In a separate bowl mix together the sour cream and mushroom soup. Pepper the chicken breasts and pour the sour cream and soup mixture over them. Bake uncovered for 3 hours.
Serves 4.

Lela Hacker Dawson
Cousin of Elvis Presley

★ LOVING ARMS LOW-FAT ★ CHICKEN CASSEROLE

1½	**to 2 pounds cooked chicken breast meat (grilled or boiled), cut into pieces**
½	**to 1 pound cooked spaghetti, drained**
1	**10¾-ounce can low-fat cream of broccoli or cream of chicken soup**
1	**10¾-ounce can chicken broth**
1	**12-ounce can Ro-tel tomatoes**
1	**16-ounce package shredded fat-free cheese**

Preheat the oven to 400°. In a casserole dish, alternate chicken and spaghetti until the pan is about three-fourths full. Pour the soup, broth, and tomatoes over the chicken and spaghetti. Stir enough to mix the ingredients. Sprinkle the cheese over top. Bake for 20 to 30 minutes. The amount of chicken you use will vary depending on the size of the dish and servings. The length of cooking time will depend on the depth of the dish.
Serve 6 to 8.

Melanie Maksim
Bavaria, Germany

★ CHICKEN DELICIOUS ★

6   **tablespoons butter**
½   **cup olive oil**
1½ **pounds chicken cutlets**
1   **cup all-purpose flour**
1½ **cups chicken broth**
2   **lemons, thinly sliced**
     Parsley

In a large skillet melt 3 teaspoons of the butter and all of the oil. Dredge the cutlets in the flour. Brown the chicken and remove from the pan. Pour ¾ cup broth into the skillet. Cook over high heat, stirring constantly, and reduce for 3 minutes.

Add the chicken to the skillet. Add ½ cup of the broth. Place the slices of 1 lemon on the chicken. Cover and simmer for 15 minutes. Move the chicken to a platter. Add the remaining ¼ cup of broth, the remaining butter, and the juice of ½ lemon to the skillet. Simmer until it thickens a bit. Pour over the chicken. Serve with rice, and garnish with parsley and the remaining lemon slices.
Serves 4.

Tim Mitchell
Cobourg, Ontario

Charlie Hodge, right-hand man for Elvis, and Nash Presley Pritchett.

★ CITY BY NIGHT CHICKEN ★

4	cloves garlic, minced
3	teaspoons parsley
2	tablespoons French-style mustard
2	chicken breasts, halved
4	drumsticks
	Pepper
5	or 6 medium onions, quartered
½	cup white wine
2	tablespoons soy sauce
1	tablespoon olive oil
¼	cup vegetable oil
2	tablespoons all-purpose flour

In a small bowl combine the garlic, parsley, and mustard until a paste forms. Paint the paste onto the chicken. Sprinkle the chicken with pepper. Place the chicken in a bowl with the onions. In a small bowl mix the wine, soy sauce, and olive oil. Pour into the bowl, cover, and refrigerate overnight. The next day turn the chicken over.

In a skillet heat the vegetable oil. Cook the onions until they are limp. Remove the onions and set them aside. Pat all-purpose flour on the chicken and brown in the same skillet until crisp. Set the chicken aside. Add the remaining flour to the skillet and stir until smooth and fawn-colored. Combine the marinade with enough water to make 2 cups and bring to a boil. Lower the heat and cook about 3 minutes until thickened. Add the chicken and onions, and simmer about 45 minutes until done.

Serves 4 to 6.

Jennifer Mitchell
Cobourg, Ontario

ON JANUARY 9, 1971, THE JAYCEES PRESENTED ELVIS WITH ONE OF THE "TEN OUTSTANDING YOUNG MEN OF AMERICA" AWARDS.

★ KENNY'S CHICKEN ★

6 tablespoons butter
½ cup olive oil
1½ pounds chicken cutlets
½ cup all-purpose flour
1½ cups chicken broth
2 lemons
Parsley

In a large skillet melt 3 teaspoons of the butter and all of the oil. Dredge the cutlets in the flour. Brown the chicken and remove from the pan. Pour ¾ cup broth into the skillet. Cook over high heat, stirring constantly, and reduce for 3 minutes.

Add the chicken to the skillet. Add ½ cup of the broth. Place the slices of 1 lemon on the chicken. Cover and simmer for 15 minutes. Move the chicken to a platter. Add the remaining ¼ cup of broth, the remaining butter, and the juice of ½ lemon to the skillet. Simmer until it thickens a bit. Pour over the chicken. Serve with rice, and garnish with parsley and the remaining lemon slices.

Serves 4 to 6.

Jackie Hacker Coleman
Cousin of Elvis Presley

Seated are Elvis's aunt Nash Presley Pritchett (left) and her daughter Susie. Standing are Nash's other daughter, Donna, and Presley family cousin Edie Hand.

★ RAISED ON ROCK ORANGE CHICKEN ★

2	to 3 pounds chicken, cut up
2	eggs, slightly beaten
⅓	cup orange juice
1	cup fine dry breadcrumbs
1	teaspoon paprika
1	teaspoon shredded orange peel
1	teaspoon salt
6	tablespoons butter

Preheat the oven to 400°. In a medium bowl combine the eggs and orange juice. Dip the chicken pieces into the bowl and coat with the mixture. In a large bowl combine the breadcrumbs, paprika, orange peel, and salt. In a large, shallow baking pan melt the butter in a 400° oven. Remove the pan from the oven, and turn the chicken in the butter to coat. Arrange the chicken skin side down (don't crowd). Bake for 30 minutes. Turn the chicken and bake 30 minutes more. If necessary, cover with foil for the last 10 minutes. Serve with Stuck on You Orange Stuffing.

Serves 6.

Shirley Beattie
Presley-Ites Fan Club
Orlando, Florida

Elvis at center stage performs with the Jordanaires in the 1957 film Loving You.
The Jordanaires (left to right) are: Ray Walker, Hoyt Hawkins, Neil Matthews, and Gordon Stoker.

★ GIVE ME THE RIGHT GOLDEN CHICKEN ★

4   boneless chicken breasts
     Oregano to taste
     Pepper to taste
2   10¾-ounce cans golden mushroom
     soup
1   1-pound bag shredded Cheddar
     cheese

Preheat the oven to 300°. Coat a baking dish with cooking spray. Place the chicken breasts in the dish. Sprinkle oregano and pepper over the chicken. Pour both cans of golden mushroom soup over the chicken. Generously sprinkle the shredded Cheddar cheese over the top. Bake for 2 hours. Serve with rice.

   Serves 4.

Rose-Ann Bernett
Canadian National Elvis Tribute Fan Club

Match the Plot with the Title of the Elvis Movie (Part Two)

1.	*Change of Habit*	A.	Gambler hits winning streak with lucky redhead by his side
2.	*Clambake*	B.	Guide turns fisherman and is torn between nightclub singer and rich girl
3.	*Easy Come, Easy Go*	C.	New Orleans schoolboy/club singer tangles with hoodlums
4.	*Flaming Star*	D.	Publicist turns gas station attendant into singing star
5.	*Frankie & Johnny*	E.	Texas oil heir swaps places with water-skiing instructor
6.	*Girl Happy*	F.	Half-breed youth must choose between white settlers and his mother's Indian tribe
7.	*Girls! Girls! Girls!*	G.	Rodeo cowboy finds work at health ranch
8.	*Kid Galahad*	H.	Doctor practicing in ghetto falls for a nurse, not knowing she is a nun
9.	*King Creole*	I.	Half-breed attempts to raise government aid for folks on reservation
10.	*Kissin' Cousins*	J.	Frogman dives for buried treasure
11.	*Loving You*	K.	Singer baby-sits mobster's daughter in Ft. Lauderdale
12.	*Paradise Hawaiian Style*	L.	Army officer deals with hillbillies over land for missile base
13.	*Spinout*	M.	Three women set their hearts on the same guy, a racer/singer
14.	*Stay Away, Joe*	N.	Garage mechanic swaps grease pit for boxing ring
15.	*Tickle Me*	O.	Former airline pilot turns tour guide

ANSWERS: 1. H, 2. E, 3. J, 4. F, 5. A, 6. K, 7. B, 8. N, 9. C, 10. L, 11. D, 12. O, 13. M, 14. I, 15. G.

★ COME WHAT MAY CHICKEN ★ WITH GOLDEN MUSHROOM SAUCE

1	medium onion, thinly sliced
1	tablespoon butter or margarine
4	boneless and skinless chicken breasts
2	10¾-ounce cans golden mushroom soup
	Dash steak seasoning sauce
½	cup white wine or chicken broth
	Salt and pepper to taste

Preheat the oven to 350°. In a heavy pan melt the butter and sauté the onions until translucent. Add the chicken breasts and brown lightly. Add the soup, steak sauce, and wine or the broth. Cover tightly and place in the oven. Bake for 45 minutes to 1 hour. Serve over cooked white rice with the sauce.

Serves 4.

Francine and Cecil Blackwood
The Blackwood Brothers

Stacy Aaron Early (Elvis's cousin and namesake and son of Donna and Buddy Early) with bride Leigh Ann on their wedding day, May 20, 1995.

★ FOOLS FALL IN LOVE FRICASSEED CHICKEN ★ ITALIAN-STYLE

2½ **pounds chicken**
¼ **cup seasoned flour**
3 **tablespoons vegetable oil**
1 **teaspoon rosemary**
1 **teaspoon garlic**
2 **tablespoons olive oil**
⅓ **cup wine vinegar**

Dredge the chicken pieces in the flour. In a large skillet heat the oil and brown the chicken. Discard the oil and wipe the skillet clean. Mix the rosemary and garlic. Heat the olive oil and return the chicken to the pan. Add the rosemary and garlic. Add the vinegar, cover, and cook on low for 45 minutes to 1 hour. If it cooks dry, add a little water.
   Serves 4 to 6.

Charles Mooney
London, England

Brothers Stacy and Jamie Early (cousins of Elvis) on Stacy's wedding day.

★  Mexico Chicken ★

1   ½-pound bag tortilla chips, crushed
3   10-ounce cans chicken
2   10¾-ounce cans cream of chicken
       soup
1   cup sour cream
1   6-ounce can chopped green chilies
1   tablespoon chopped onion
1   cup shredded Cheddar cheese

Preheat the oven to 425°. Place the crushed tortilla chips in a casserole dish. Place the chicken on top of the crushed chips. In a large bowl combine the soup, sour cream, chilies, and onion, and pour over the chips. Sprinkle the cheese on top. Bake until the cheese melts.
       Serves 6 to 8.

Mary Tom Speer Reid
The Speer Family

★  Southern Fried Chicken ★

1   fryer, cut up
1½ cups milk
     Salt and pepper to taste
     All-purpose flour
1   tablespoon paprika
     Dash cayenne pepper (if desired)
2   teaspoons garlic powder or salt
½   cup cooking oil

In a covered pan or plastic bag, soak the cut-up chicken in milk for 45 to 60 minutes in the refrigerator. Turn once or twice to coat all sides of the chicken. Mix the dry ingredients together. Remove the chicken from the milk and roll in the flour mixture. Place each piece separated on waxed paper. Let sit on the paper for 5 minutes. Heat the oil in an iron skillet. When the oil is hot enough for frying, roll each chicken piece in the flour mixture once more and fry. Drain the chicken on a brown paper bag.
       Serves 2 to 4.

Ann Morrison
Folkston, Georgia
Elvis Always Fan Club

★ THE BEST FRIED CHICKEN ★

1   **whole chicken**
2   **to 3 cups self-rising flour**
1   **teaspoon salt**
½   **cup buttermilk**
¼   **cup oil**

When you buy fresh chicken to fry, I recommend that you immediately skin it and rinse it well. Place the chicken in an airtight container with water, some ice, and salt. (The amount of salt depends on the amount of chicken. For 5 or 6 pieces, use 1 teaspoon of salt dissolved in water. Be careful not to get too much salt or the chicken will be salty.) Store the chicken in the refrigerator for up to 2 days, drain the water and pour buttermilk over the chicken. Return it to the refrigerator until you are ready to fry it.

Sift 2 to 3 cups of self-rising flour into a large mixing bowl. Set aside. Remove the cleaned and skinned chicken from the refrigerator. Remove the chicken from the buttermilk and place it on a platter. Let the excess buttermilk drain off. Place the drained chicken into the flour, turning to coat well and patting it on, if necessary.

In a frying pan or fryer heat the oil to approximately 350°. Place pieces of chicken in the pan. You may have to turn the heat down some, but remember that the cold chicken will cool the oil and if the oil is not hot enough, the chicken will absorb the oil and be soggy. Fry at medium-high heat for about 7 minutes. Turn chicken over and brown other side for 6 to 7 minutes. Be sure the chicken is well done.
Serves 4 to 6.

Betty Jo McMichael
Co-owner, Whistle Stop Cafe
Irondale, Alabama

ELVIS'S TUNE "G.I. BLUES" STUCK ON THE
BILLBOARD CHARTS FOR 111 WEEKS.

★ TWENTY DAYS AND TWENTY NIGHTS ★
FRIED TURKEY

8   ounces (1 cup) zesty Italian dressing, strain and set aside the seasonings
1   to 3 tablespoons steak seasoning sauce
1   to 3 tablespoons barbecue sauce
1   teaspoon hot pepper sauce
1   teaspoon lemon or lime juice
    Dash hot pepper sauce

In a large jar shake the ingredients together to mix well. Inject into turkey. Rub the seasonings from the dressings inside the cavity of the turkey. In a large fryer heat the oil to 325°. Cook 3 to 4 minutes per pound.

Serves 10.

Verna Melohn
Elvis fan

Courtesy of James Blackwood

Backstage at a gospel music convention at Ellis Auditorium in Memphis, Elvis joins the Blackwood Brothers (left to right: James Blackwood, Hovie Lister, and J. D. Sumner) for an impromptu rendition of "How Great Thou Art."

Left: *Elvis and Jimmy Velvet backstage in 1956.*

Below: *Elvis and Red West relaxing together in a hotel room in 1954.*

Right: *While in Nashville in 1960, Elvis paused from riding this motorcycle to have his picture taken.*

Below: *In the lobby of a Memphis theater with Rodonna Brock and her mother. Elvis often rented this theater so he could watch movies there with his friends.*

Left: *While on Army duty in Germany, Elvis enjoyed a tasty American hamburger.*

Below: *on location for the film G.I. Blues, for Paramount Pictures in November of 1960.*

Above: *Elvis and Priscilla at their wedding reception in Las Vegas.*

Below: *A family photo taken inside Graceland. From left to right: Elvis's grandmother ("Dodger"), Priscilla, Lisa Marie, Elvis, and Charlie Hodge.*

Left: *Elvis with fans Jeanine Paiva and her mother in front of his home at 1174 Hillcrest in Bel Air in 1969. Notice the metal gates behind them. Originally they were open, providing a view of the house; but Priscilla did not like the fans looking through them. Elvis had the gates backed by sheet metal; but he did not like this look, and the sheet metal did not last very long.*

Below: *Elvis posing with a fan outside the gates of 1174 Hillcrest. At the time he was growing a beard for his part in the movie Charro! He is holding a small toy that a fan gave him for Lisa Marie.*

Right: *Handing an autographed photo back to a fan in front of Elvis's home at 1174 Hillcrest. With him in the car is Red West.*

Below: *Signing an autograph for a fan in the hallway of the International Hotel in Las Vegas, September 1970.*

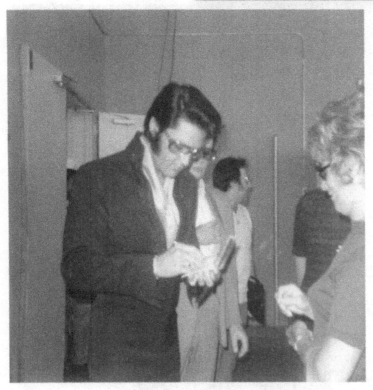

Left: *This photo was taken outside his home at 1174 Hillcrest on March 9, 1964. Elvis was signing autographs for his fans.*

Below: *A quiet moment. Location unknown.*

Right: *A scene from the Paramount Pictures film* Roustabout.

Below: *On location for the movie* Blue Hawaii. *Elvis and his co-stars were riding their horses in Ala Moana Park.*

★ EASY COME, EASY GO CHICKEN POT PIE ★

2   cups cooked chicken
2   10¾-ounce cans cream of chicken
      soup
2   10-ounce cans mixed vegetables
1   teaspoon minced onion
      Salt and pepper to taste
1   8-ounce can refrigerator biscuits

Preheat the oven to 350°. In a round casserole dish combine the chicken, soup, vegetables, onion, and salt and pepper to taste. Cover and bake for 1 hour.

Remove the cover and place the biscuits on the chicken mixture. Return to the oven and bake uncovered for 12 minutes or until the biscuits are browned.

Serves 4.

Edie Hand
Cousin of Elvis Presley

ELVIS'S FIRST LOVE WAS GOSPEL MUSIC.
HE AND HIS FAMILY AND FRIENDS, LIKE
JAMES BLACKWOOD OF THE BLACKWOOD
BROTHERS, WOULD SIT ON THE PORCH FOR
HOURS HARMONIZING ON GOSPEL TUNES.
IN FACT, EARLY ON, THAT'S WHAT ELVIS
WANTED TO BE—A GOSPEL SINGER.

★ ASK ME CHICKEN CASSEROLE ★

3	cups chopped cooked chicken
1	10-ounce can mixed vegetables
1	cup grated cheese
1	cup chopped onion
1	10¾-ounce can cream of potato soup
1	20-ounce box buttery rich crackers, crushed
2	tablespoons margarine

Preheat the oven to 350°. In a baking dish combine the chicken, mixed vegetables, cheese, onion, and soup. Top with crushed crackers. Drizzle melted margarine over the top. Bake for 30 minutes.

Serves 4.

Marie Isbell
Sylacauga, Alabama

PLANE VIEW—Elvis arrives in style. At the lower left is his close friend Red West.

★ DOUBLE TROUBLE CHICKEN AND DUMPLINGS ★

1　2½- to 3-pound broiler-fryer, cut up
　　and skinned
1　tablespoon salt
1　teaspoon pepper
　　Plain pastry, chilled
¾　cup milk
½　cup (1 stick) margarine

Place the chicken in a saucepan and cover with water. Add the salt and pepper and bring to a boil. Cover, reduce the heat, and simmer for 45 minutes to 1 hour or until the chicken is very tender. Remove the chicken from the broth and let it cool. Bone the chicken and cut it into very small pieces.

Place the chilled pastry on a lightly floured surface and roll thin. Cut it into 3-inch strips. Bring the broth to a boil and add milk and margarine. Drop the pastry strips into the boiling broth. Reduce the heat and cook 6 to 8 minutes longer. Uncover and add diced chicken. Cook until thoroughly heated.

Serves 4 to 6.

Betty Jo McMichael
Co-owner, Whistle Stop Cafe
Irondale, Alabama

Elvis and a captive audience in Nashville.

★ SHOPPIN' AROUND SHRIMP GUMBO ★

¼ **cup (½ stick) margarine or butter**

2 **medium onions, sliced**

1 **medium green pepper, cut into thin strips**

2 **cloves garlic, crushed**

2 **tablespoons all-purpose flour**

3 **cups water**

1 **tablespoon powdered instant beef bouillon**

1 **teaspoon salt**

¼ **teaspoon pepper**

½ **teaspoon red pepper sauce**

1 **bay leaf**

1 **16-ounce can okra, drained, or 1 10-ounce package frozen cut okra, thawed**

1 **6-ounce can tomato paste**

1 **10-ounce can whole tomatoes, undrained**

1½ **pounds fresh or frozen raw shrimp, thawed**

3 **cups hot cooked rice**

¼ **cup snipped parsley**

In a Dutch oven melt the butter and sauté the onions, green pepper, and garlic over low heat until the onions are tender. Stir in the flour and cook over low heat, stirring constantly until bubbly. Remove the pan from the heat and stir in the remaining ingredients except for the shrimp, rice, and parsley. Break up the tomatoes with a fork. Heat to boiling. Reduce the heat and simmer uncovered for 45 minutes, stirring occasionally.

Peel the shrimp. Make a shallow slit lengthwise down the back of each shrimp, wash out any sand, and devein. Stir the shrimp into the tomato mixture, cover, and simmer about 5 minutes until the shrimp are white. Remove the bay leaf. Serve the gumbo over rice, and sprinkle with parsley.

Serves 6.

Marlene Nunez
Elvis Country Fan Club

★ LOBSTER KING CREOLE ★

2   lobsters to a pot
3   to 4 quarts water
1   tablespoon salt per quart water

Bring the water to a boil and add the salt. Grasp each live lobster, one at a time, by cupping your hand around the back and plunging it head-first into the boiling water. Cover the pot and after the water returns to a boil, cook for 5 to 6 minutes per pound. Test for doneness. Pull on an antenna on the head. If it comes out easily, it is done. Drain the lobsters and serve hot.

Variation: For steamed lobster, pour 1 inch of water into a large kettle and bring to a boil over high heat. Add the lobsters, cover, and steam for 15 minutes.

Stacie Benes
Washington, D.C.

Elvis's favorite horse was Rising Sun. Earl Pritchett made sure Elvis's regal palomino was well cared for.

★ SPANISH EYES STEW ★

1	tablespoon oil
½	cup chopped onion
½	cup chopped celery
½	cup chopped green pepper
4	chicken breasts, cooked and cubed
1	14½-ounce can tomato chunks
1	10-ounce can diced Ro-tel tomatoes
1	8-ounce can tomato sauce
1	15-ounce can sliced potatoes
1	10¾-ounce can cream of celery soup
1	10¾-ounce can cream of chicken soup
1	16-ounce can pork and beans
1	11-ounce can kernel corn
1	15-ounce can lima beans
½	package Southwestern herb mix
	Salt and pepper to taste

In a large pot heat the oil and sauté the onion, celery, and green pepper. Add the remaining ingredients and cook for 15 to 20 minutes. **Serves 10 to 12.**

Rochelle Reed Brunson
Angleton, Texas

Rochelle Brunson and son Barkley visit Elvis Presley's birthplace in Tupelo, Mississippi, on Christmas Day 1997.

★ STEAMROLLER BLUES BRUNSWICK STEW ★

1   pork roast
2   whole chickens (white meat)
1   beef roast or stew meat
8   medium onions, finely chopped
9   large potatoes, chopped
20 ounces ketchup
4   20-ounce cans tomatoes
    Black pepper to taste
    Red pepper to taste
    Salt to taste
2   15-ounce cans butter beans
3   15-ounce cans cream-style corn

In a large pot cook the meat. Remove the meat from the bones and chop fine. Cook the onions and potatoes in the broth, using just enough to cover. In a large pot combine all of the ingredients and cook without a lid for 2 hours, stirring often. Add more broth if needed.

Serve with barbecue, cole slaw, pickles, and bread, if desired. This freezes well.

Serves 10 to 12.

Nash Presley Pritchett
Aunt of Elvis Presley

DURING HIS MANY YEARS AS A RECORDING ARTIST ELVIS RECEIVED FOURTEEN GRAMMY NOMINATIONS, BUT HE WON ONLY THREE GRAMMYS, AND ALL WERE FOR GOSPEL TUNES: BEST SACRED PERFORMANCE, "HOW GREAT THOU ART" (1967); BEST INSPIRATIONAL PERFORMANCE, "HE TOUCHED ME" (1972); AND BEST INSPIRATIONAL PERFORMANCE, "HOW GREAT THOU ART" (1974).

★ A BOY LIKE ME BEEF STEW ★

2	pounds lean stew beef, cut into 1-inch cubes
1	teaspoon salt
1	teaspoon garlic powder
1	teaspoon seasoned salt
1	teaspoon black pepper
3	or 4 large potatoes, cubed
3	large onions, quartered
2	14½-ounce cans whole or diced tomatoes, undrained
2	15½-ounce cans tomato sauce

Rinse the stew meat and place in a large boiler. Add the spices and water to cover. Bring to a boil. Reduce the heat and simmer for 1 hour or until the meat is tender.

In a separate pot cook the potatoes and onions in water. When the potatoes and onions are tender, drain in a colander and add to the meat. Add the tomatoes and tomato sauce, stirring well. Simmer for 25 to 30 minutes.

Serves 8.

Betty Jo McMichael
Co-owner, Whistle Stop Cafe
Irondale, Alabama

Elvis on TV

Match the correct date to the TV show.
(Two of the TV events were on the same day)

1.	Dance Party	A.	March 5, 1955
2.	The Ed Sullivan Show	B.	March 19, 1955
3.	ELVIS	C.	January 28, 1956
4.	Elvis Aloha From Hawaii	D.	April 3, 1956
5.	Holiday Hop	E.	June 20, 1956
6.	Hy Gardner Calling	F.	July 1, 1956
7.	Grand Prize Saturday Night Jamboree	G.	July 1, 1956
8.	Louisiana Hayride	H.	September 9, 1956
9.	The Milton Berle Show	I.	December 31, 1956
10.	Stage Show	J.	May 12, 1960
11.	The Steve Allen Show	K.	December 3, 1968
12.	Welcome Home Elvis	L.	January 14, 1973

ANSWERS: 1. E, 2. H, 3. K, 4. L, 5. I, 6. F, 7. B, 8. A, 9. D, 10. C, 11. G, 12. J

★ RETURN TO SUKIYAKI (JAPANESE BEEF STEW) ★

Cabbage (American or Chinese)
Spring onions
Carrots
Bean sprouts
Water chestnuts
1   **Tender cut beef (chicken, pork, or**
     shrimp may be substituted)
Soy sauce
¼   **teaspoon cooking oil**
¼   **teaspoon dry mustard**
½   **teaspoon ground ginger**

Chop all of the vegetables except the carrots. Sliver the carrots with potato peeler. Cut the meat into small, thin pieces. Marinate the meat in soy sauce for 30 minutes before cooking. Heat a wok or large frying pan to a moderate heat. Pour in the oil and 1 tablespoon of soy sauce. When the liquids in the wok start to bubble, put in the meat. Brown the meat on all sides. Put the cabbage on top of the meat. Cover and cook until the cabbage begins to soften, but is not soggy. Sprinkle with the dry mustard and ginger. Add all additional vegetables with the bean sprouts on top. Cover and cook at low heat for 3 minutes. Stir all the ingredients and turn the heat to warm. Serve at this temperature over white rice accompanied by a cucumber salad and hot tea.

Seiko Yagyu Machida
Tokyo, Japan

Gary Peppers, a close friend of Elvis, visits Dodger Presley, who's sitting in her favorite chair in her room at Graceland.

★ BLUE EYES BEEF AND VEGETABLE STIR-FRY ★

¾ **pound boneless beef sirloin steak**

½ **cup beef broth**

2 **tablespoons soy sauce**

1 **tablespoon cornstarch**

2 **tablespoons sugar**

½ **teaspoon ground ginger**

3 **tablespoons vegetable oil**

½ **pound green beans, cut in half diagonally**

2 **small onions, cut into wedges**

¼ **pound mushrooms, sliced**

Freeze the steak until firm enough to slice easily. Trim and discard any excess fat from the meat. Cut the steak crosswise into thin slices. In a small bowl combine the broth, soy sauce, cornstarch, sugar, and ginger. Heat a medium-sized skillet and add 2 tablespoons of the oil, the beans, and the onions. Cook, stirring with a slotted spoon until crispy and tender. Add the mushrooms and stir-fry until tender. Remove the vegetables from the heat and place in a bowl.

Add the remaining oil to the skillet and stir-fry the beef over high heat until just well browned. Remove the pan from the heat and place on a plate. Add the cornstarch mixture to the skillet. Heat to boiling, and then return the vegetables to the skillet. Heat until hot, stir in the beef, and serve immediately.

Serves 6.

Betty Jo McMichael
Co-owner, Whistle Stop Cafe
Irondale, Alabama

THERE IS AN ELVIS PRESLEY BOULEVARD IN MEMPHIS, AN ELVIS PRESLEY PLAZA IN MEMPHIS NEAR BEALE STREET, AND AN ELVIS PRESLEY CHAPEL IN TUPELO. OLD SALTILLO ROAD IN TUPELO, WHERE ELVIS WAS BORN, WAS RENAMED ELVIS PRESLEY BOULEVARD, AND THE AREA IN TUPELO WHERE ELVIS WAS BORN WAS RENAMED ELVIS PRESLEY HEIGHTS.

★ RIP IT UP BEEF TIPS AND RICE ★

3 pounds lean sirloin tip roast, cut
   into small pieces
1 quart water
1 medium onion, finely chopped
1 bell pepper, finely chopped
¼ cup Worcestershire sauce
¼ cup soy sauce
1 teaspoon garlic powder
1 teaspoon seasoned salt
1 teaspoon black pepper
2 tablespoons self-rising flour
1 cup water
8 cups cooked rice

In a Dutch oven combine the cooked beef, 1 quart of water, onion, bell pepper, Worcestershire sauce, and soy sauce. Place over medium-high heat and bring to a boil. Add the garlic powder, seasoned salt, and black pepper. Reduce the heat and simmer for about 1 hour.

In a small bowl mix the self-rising flour and 1 cup of water and stir into the hot mixture. Cook over medium heat until thickened.

Serves 6.

Betty Jo McMichael
Co-owner, Whistle Stop Cafe
Irondale, Alabama

★ BAMA BEEF AND RICE ★

1 pound ground beef
2 tablespoons butter
1 medium onion, diced
1 medium green pepper, chopped
½ cup converted rice
1 teaspoon salt
¼ teaspoon pepper
1 6-ounce can tomato paste
2 cups hot water

Preheat the oven to 350°. In a heavy 10-inch skillet cook the beef just until it loses its redness. Crumble the meat with a fork and place it in a buttered casserole dish. In a separate skillet melt 1 tablespoon of the butter and cook the onion and green pepper until wilted. Add the vegetables to the beef. In the same skillet cook the rice in the remaining butter, stirring constantly until golden. Add the rice to the beef and season with salt and pepper. Stir together the tomato paste and water to blend. Pour over the beef mixture. Do not stir. Bake about 1 hour until the rice is tender. The tomato mixture will be on top.

Serves 6.

Marsha Kinsaul
Dora, Alabama

★ GIRLS! GIRLS! GOULASH! ★

2	teaspoons butter
1	cup chopped onion
1	cup chopped green pepper
1	pound ground beef
1	cup raw rice
1	16-ounce can whole tomatoes
1	tablespoon chili powder
	Salt and pepper to taste

Preheat the oven to 350°. In a skillet melt the butter and sauté the onion and bell pepper until soft. Add the ground beef and cook, stirring constantly, until brown. Add the rice, tomatoes, chili powder, and salt and pepper. Transfer the mixture to a baking dish and bake for 1 hour.

Serves 4 to 6.

Jean Busby
Elvis Country Fan Club

Edie Hand and Nash Presley Pritchett pose by a fence
at the back of Graceland in 1976.

★ PROUD MARY PORK SAUSAGE ★ AND WILD RICE CASSEROLE

1½ pounds regular sausage
1½ pounds spicy sausage
1 cup chopped celery
½ cup chopped onion
2 6-ounce packages long grain and
   wild rice
1 2-ounce package dry chicken
   noodle soup
5 cups hot water

Preheat the oven to 350°. In a skillet partially cook the sausage, celery, and onion. Drain off the excess fat. Stir in the rice and soup. Transfer to a baking dish and add the water. Mix and cover. Bake for 45 to 60 minutes or until the rice is tender.

Serves 6.

Rochelle Reid Brunson
Angleton, Texas

Aunt Delta is seen here walking Edmund II on the Graceland grounds.

★ SUMMER KISSES PORK AND SAUERKRAUT ★ CASSEROLE

2	pounds country-style ribs
1	medium onion, diced
14	ounces sauerkraut
1	apple, diced and peeled
1	teaspoon caraway seeds
2	tablespoons brown sugar
	Salt and pepper
2	cups hot chicken stock

Preheat the oven to 350°. In a large skillet brown the ribs and the onion. Remove the fat from the skillet.

Add the remaining ingredients. Transfer the mixture to a casserole dish. Cover and bake for 1 hour. Add water if needed.

Serves 4.

Margie Best
Chicago, Illinois

Elvis's uncle Vester in his security guard uniform at the gates of Graceland.

★ SPRING FEVER PORK STEW ★

2	pounds lean pork, shoulder or neck
1	teaspoon salt
½	teaspoon pepper
2	tablespoons shortening or oil
1	small onion, chopped
4	green onions, chopped
2	ribs celery, chopped
7	carrots, diced
2	tablespoons all-purpose flour
3	sprigs parsley
1	bay leaf
½	teaspoon whole thyme
3	whole cloves
6	medium potatoes

Have the butcher cut the meat into serving pieces. Sprinkle the meat with salt and pepper. In a large heavy skillet heat the shortening or oil and brown the meat well on all sides. Add the onions, celery, and carrots to the meat and brown slightly. Sprinkle with flour and then add enough water to cover. Mix well and bring to a boil. Add the parsley, bay leaf, thyme, and cloves to the stew. Cover securely and simmer over low heat for 25 minutes.

While the stew is simmering, peel the potatoes. Cut the potatoes into 1½-inch cubes. Add the potatoes to the stew and continue cooking slowly until the meat is tender when pierced with a fork. This should take about 45 minutes.

When the stew is done, skim out the parsley, bay leaf, thyme, and cloves.

Serves 6.

Edie Hand
Cousin of Elvis Presley

DECEMBER 21, 1970, PRESIDENT RICHARD M. NIXON PRESENTED ELVIS WITH AN HONORARY NARCOTICS BUREAU BADGE DURING A PRIVATE MEETING AT THE WHITE HOUSE.

★ EL TORO CHILIES RELLEÑOS CASSEROLE ★

2	**4-ounce cans green chilies**
4	**cups grated Cheddar cheese**
3	**cups milk**
3	**eggs, beaten**
1	**cup packaged biscuit mix**
1	**teaspoon salt**

Preheat the oven to 350°. In a well-oiled 9 x 13-inch baking dish place the peppers in a single layer. Sprinkle the grated cheese over the peppers. In a large bowl mix together the milk, eggs, biscuit mix, and salt. Pour over the cheese and peppers. Bake for 45 minutes to 1 hour. **Serves 4.**

Verna Melohn
Elvis fan

★ SNAKE BITE CHILI ★

2	**pounds deer meat (tender cut)**
1	**can rattlesnake meat**
2	**tablespoons butter**
10	**jalapeño peppers**
4	**cups pinto beans, drained**
4	**large tomatoes, skinned and halved**
2	**tablespoons chili powder**
¼	**teaspoon crushed red pepper**
2	**cups water**

Brown the meat in the butter. Drain and put in a crock pot or large pot. Slice the jalapeño peppers and add to the pot. Put all the other ingredients in the pot. Simmer for 2 to 4 hours, stirring every ½ hour. **Serves 4 to 6.**

Sylvia Delap
Malinda, Kenya

Side Dishes

★ SOUTHERN GRITS ★

2 cups cold water
Pinch salt
1 cup grits, washed
½ cup milk
Butter (optional)
½ cup grated cheese (optional)

Add the pinch of salt to the cold water. Pour into the top of a double boiler and add the cup of grits. Place over simmering water and cook for approximately 1 hour.

As the grits begin to thicken, beat often and add water if needed. Toward the end of the cooking period, add the milk and beat again. Allow the mixture to thicken.

Those who mill the grits will tell you that the longer they cook, the better they are and that the secret is in the beating. In the South, we refer to "swimmin' the grits", when we wash them, and if you let them set overnight in the water, they'll cook better and faster.

A lump of butter added and beaten into the grits just before they are removed from the heat tastes great. Plus, ½ cup of strong, shaved cheese added to the above pot of grits, blended and cooked a few minutes, and served along with scrambled eggs, bacon, and biscuits makes for just about the best breakfast a man or woman could want!
Serves 4 to 6.

Edie Hand
Cousin of Elvis Presley

★ ALABAMA GRITS CASSEROLE ★

3	cups boiling water
¾	cup coarse grits (not the quick type)
1	teaspoon salt
6	tablespoons (¾ stick) butter
½	pound American cheese, cubed
½	teaspoon hot pepper sauce
½	teaspoon seasoning salt
2	eggs, beaten with a fork before adding

Put the water in a saucepan and throw in the grits. Bring the water to a boil and cook the grits for 10 to 15 minutes, stirring frequently.

Add the salt, butter, and American cheese. Stir well and let the cheese melt. Add the hot pepper sauce, seasoning salt, and eggs. Stir well and pour into a baking dish. Preheat the oven to 250° and bake for 1 hour.

This is an excellent dish to make ahead of time and place in the refrigerator. Bake it when you are ready to serve.

Serves 6.

Darolyn Arrington
Montgomery, Alabama

The Graceland Menagerie

Elvis loved animals of all kinds. He had numerous pets while growing up and compiled a full menagerie at Graceland. Elvis's favorite horse was a palomino named Rising Sun.

When Elvis got Rising Sun, he had to make sure his grandmother Dodger got to see the steed. So he rode the horse up to the window, but that wasn't good enough for Elvis. He ended up bringing the horse into the house for Dodger to get an up close and personal look. Rising Sun chose that moment to relieve himself right on the floor of the house.

Elvis had about fourteen horses, so that his friends could ride along with him, and he had a pony for Lisa Marie. The steeds included Bear, a prize-winning Tennessee walking horse; Domino, Priscilla's quarter horse; and a mare named Ingram, which he kept at the Circle G Ranch.

Elvis had a passel of dogs. His first was a mongrel named Lboy. Perhaps his favorite was Getlow, a chow who thought he owned Graceland. The dog would not ride in the back seat of Elvis's car. The hound would take his place in the front seat, and anyone who was going riding with Elvis had to sit in the back seat.

Eventually Getlow became seriously ill. So Elvis flew girlfriend Linda Thompson and the dog to Boston to see a veterinarian at a clinic that specialized in the disease afflicting Getlow. But it was to no avail. Getlow died and Elvis cried over the loss of his beloved chow.

There were many other dogs in Elvis's life. Among these were Sweet Pea, a dog he gave to Gladys in 1956; two Great Danes named Snoopy and Brutus; two poodles named Stuff and Spontaneous Combustion; a Great Pyranees named Muffin; a puppy named Honey that he gave Priscilla for a Christmas gift in 1962; a basset hound named Sherlock; a maltese named Widdlon; a collie named Allie Baba; a bulldog named Boston Blackie; and there was Edmund, a Pomeranian, at Graceland in 1977.

And then there was Scatter, a forty-pound chimp. Scatter was a mess. He would chase the girls. The guys in the Memphis Mafia would dress him up in women's clothes for laughs. He would roam around the house but never into Grandma's room. She wouldn't allow that.

★ BY AND BY BAKED CHEESE GRITS ★

1½ **cups quick-cooking grits**
¾ **cup butter, soft**
4½ **cups grated sharp Cheddar cheese**
6 **eggs, separated**
6 **tablespoons light cream**
 Few dashes steak seasoning sauce
 Salt and pepper to taste

Preheat the oven to 350°. Cook the grits according to the package instructions until they are thick and smooth. Stir in the butter. Add 3 cups of the cheese, the slightly beaten egg yolks, cream, steak seasoning sauce, and seasonings. Beat the egg whites until they are stiff, fold in the grits mixture, and spoon into 2 greased 1½-quart casserole dishes (this can be done a day ahead). Bake for 20 to 30 minutes.

Sprinkle the top with the remaining cheese. Return to the oven and bake for 15 minutes longer.
Serves 6 to 8.

Jane Lynn
Birmingham, Alabama

NUMBER ONE SUN—Elvis is seen here riding his favorite horse, Rising Sun, at Graceland.

★ CINDY, CINDY CHEESE GRITS ★

3   cups cooked grits

2   eggs, beaten

⅓   cup milk

1   teaspoon salt

1   teaspoon garlic powder

¼   cup (½ stick) margarine or butter

1   cup grated cheese

Preheat the oven to 350°. In a large bowl combine the grits, eggs, milk, salt, and garlic powder. Mix together well. Cut the margarine into bits and stir into the grits mixture. Add ⅔ cup of the cheese and pour into a greased baking dish. Sprinkle the remaining cheese on top. Bake for 30 minutes.

    Serves 6.

Lea Stotler
Lake Geneva, Wisconsin

Nash Presley Pritchett at Graceland.

★ GREEN, GREEN BEANS OF HOME ★

2   pounds fresh snap, pole, or string
    beans
2   ounces salt pork
1   teaspoon salt
1   medium onion, peeled
1   medium russet potato, peeled

Break the tips off the ends of the beans, and wash and drain them. Cut an X on top of the salt pork, cutting to but not through the rind. In a large heavy saucepan combine the beans, salt pork, salt, onion, and potato. Add water to barely cover. Bring the water to a boil. Cover, reduce the heat, and simmer for 1 hour.

Serves 6 to 8.

Betty Jo McMichael
Co-owner, Whistle Stop Cafe
Irondale, Alabama

This is the house where Elvis was born in Tupelo, Mississippi.
His aunt Nash grew up in a house next door.

★ LIKE-FRESH GREEN BEANS ★

1 **15-ounce can green beans**
   Dash salt
   Water
2 **tablespoons butter**
   Pinch sugar
   Bouillon cubes
   Dash pepper

Drain the liquid from the can. Rinse the beans thoroughly in cold water. Put them in a pan and add a dash of salt. Add enough water to cover the beans. Add the butter. Bring to a boil and boil for a few minutes. Add the bouillon cube and stir. Then add the pinch of sugar. Add the pepper before serving.

Tip: Add 1 cube of bouillon for each 2 cups of water. The secret to making them taste like fresh is the sugar.

This recipe also works for canned carrots. Chop the carrots up with a spoon to look home sliced.

Serves 4.

Charles Mooney
London, England

ELVIS WAS ON THE CONCERT TRAIL OR IN THE STUDIOS MAKING MOVIES SO MUCH OF THE TIME THAT WHEN HE WAS HOME AT GRACELAND HE LIKED TO EAT A FORMAL DINNER EVERY NIGHT, USUALLY AROUND 9 P.M., IN THE DINING ROOM. EVERYONE WOULD COME TO THE TABLE DRESSED UP IN THEIR EVENING BEST.

Elvis—ready to serve his country.

★ TOMORROW NEVER COMES SLICED GREEN ★ TOMATOES OR FRIED SQUASH

4   green tomatoes or squash
¼   cup all-purpose flour
1   cup cornmeal
     Salt and pepper
2   tablespoons vegetable oil

Cut the tomatoes or squash into slices. Mix the flour and cornmeal together in a large bowl. Add salt and pepper to taste. Roll the vegetable slices in the batter. In a skillet heat the oil. Add the battered slices and fry until brown.
     Serves 6 to 8.

Pat Early
Donna Presley Early's mother-in-law

Elvis has fun opening a gift from a fan as Debra Paget watches. This photograph was taken on the first day of filming of Elvis's first movie, Love Me Tender, in 1956.

★ TWEEDLEE-DEE GREEN TOMATO CASSEROLE ★

4	green tomatoes
½	cup shredded mild Cheddar cheese
1	cup dry breadcrumbs
2	tablespoons butter or margarine
	Dash salt and pepper

Preheat the oven to 400°. Slice the tomatoes. Layer the tomato slices, cheese, and breadcrumbs in a casserole dish and dot with butter. Sprinkle salt and pepper over the top. Cover the dish and bake for 45 minutes.

Serves 4 to 6.

Darolyn Arrington
Montgomery, Alabama

from Elvis Flick to Television (Part One)

Match the actor who worked with Elvis to the TV series they starred or co-starred in.

PLAYING COWBOYS

1.	Michael Ansara *(Harum Scarum)*	A.	*The Big Valley*
2.	Neville Brand *(Love Me Tender)*	B.	*The High Chaparral*
3.	Paul Brinegar *(Charro)*	C.	*Laredo*
4.	James Drury *(Love Me Tender)*	D.	*Law of the Plainsman*
5.	Leif Erickson *(Roustabout)*	E.	*Rawhide*
6.	Will Hutchins *(Spinout)*	F.	*Sugarfoot*
7.	John McEntire *(Flaming Star)*	G.	*The Virginian*
8.	Barbara Stanwyck *(Roustabout)*	H.	*Wagon Train*

ANSWERS: 1. D, 2. C, 3. E, 4. G, 5. B, 6. F, 7. H, 8. A

★ DOWN HOME COLLARD GREENS ★

1	head collard greens
1	ham hock
	Pepper
	Pepper vinegar

Soak and wash the collard greens in a colander. Rinse and chop the greens into 1-inch pieces. In a large pot boil water with the ham hock. Add a pinch of pepper. Drop the collards into the water and cook until limp. Serve with pepper vinegar on the side
Serves 4 to 6.

Ovaline Marchant
Vance, Alabama

★ MARY IN THE MORNING ★
MARINATED CARROTS

2	16-ounce cans carrots, drained and sliced
2	green peppers
2	medium white onions
1	10¾-ounce can tomato soup
1	teaspoon mustard
1	teaspoon steak seasoning sauce
¾	cup sugar

In a saucepan of boiling water cook the carrots until crisp and tender. Cut the peppers and onions into small wedges. Add them to the saucepan. Add the remaining ingredients, stir well, and simmer until the vegetables are tender.
Serves 4.

Babe C. Crossman
Elvis Country Fan Club

★ RISING SUN CARROTS WITH BACON ★

3   tablespoons butter or margarine
3   cups fresh carrots, sliced
    Salt and pepper
3   slices bacon, cooked and crumbled
2   tablespoons chopped parsley

In a large skillet melt the butter and sauté the carrots until they are tender. Add the salt and pepper, bacon, and parsley. Toss together and simmer for a few minutes. Serve warm.
    Serves 4.

Gerry Mitchell
Cobourg, Ontario

Elvis looking to his future as the king of rock 'n' roll.

★ FESTIVE CAULIFLOWER ★

Water

Salt

4 cups cauliflower, cut into florets

1 10¾-ounce can cream of celery
    soup

½ cup milk

½ cup shredded Cheddar cheese

⅛ teaspoon curry powder (if desired)

Dash pepper

1 cup frozen peas, thawed

½ cup diced sweet red pepper

Toasted sliced almonds

In a skillet bring ½ inch of salted water to a boil. Add the cauliflower, cover, and cook for 5 minutes or until the florets are tender-crisp. Drain and stir in the soup, milk, cheese, curry, and pepper until the mixture is smooth. Add the peas and red pepper. Cook for 5 minutes or until the vegetables are tender, stirring often. Place in a serving bowl and top with almonds.

Microwave Version: In a 2-quart microwavable casserole dish place the cauliflower in ½ inch of salted water. Cover and microwave on high for 10 minutes or until it is tender-crisp. Drain and stir in the soup, milk, cheese, curry, and pepper until smooth. Add the peas and red pepper, and cover. Microwave on high for 3 minutes or until the vegetables are tender, stirring once during the cooking. Place in a serving bowl and top with almonds.

Serves 5.

Georgann Reynolds
Elvis Country Fan Club

THERE ARE 630 ELVIS PRESLEY FAN CLUBS AROUND THE WORLD WITH 2.2 MILLION MEMBERS. THEY'RE IN PLACES LIKE TOKYO, BRUSSELS, BANGKOK, SYDNEY, AND CHINA. CURRENTLY, THE LARGEST ONE IN THE WORLD IS IN JAPAN. THE LARGEST ELVIS FAN CLUB IN AMERICA IS IN AUSTIN, TEXAS.

★ BIG BOOTS BEET GREENS ★

1   large bunch beet greens (you can
    also use turnip greens or
    spinach)
2   slices lemon
    Salt and pepper
1   tablespoon butter
1   small sweet onion, diced

Wash the greens and put them into a pan with the water that clings to the greens and cover. Add the lemon and salt and pepper. Bring to a boil. Reduce the heat and cook for 3 or 4 minutes. Drain well, and save the broth for soup. Dice the red stems and coarsely chop the greens. Combine and toss with the butter and onion. Season to taste. Serve hot with corn bread.

Serves 4 to 6.

Linda Sue Hacker Whitaker
Cousin of Elvis Presley

Cousins Donna Presley Early (left) and Edie Hand (right) visit with Colonel Tom Parker's daughter-in-law Sandra Ross at an Elvis fan convention in Orlando, Florida.

★ Rags to Riches Red Cabbage ★

¼ **cup (½ stick) butter**

4 **cups shredded red cabbage**

2 **tart apples, thinly sliced**

½ **cup water**

¼ **cup fresh lemon juice**

½ **teaspoon caraway seeds**

½ **teaspoon salt**

⅛ **teaspoon pepper**

In a 2-quart saucepan with a cover, melt the butter. Add the remaining ingredients and stir lightly. Cover and cook 10 to 15 minutes or until the cabbage is just tender.

Serves 6.

Helen and Doyle Hood
Cousin of Elvis Presley

Family members gathered for the wedding of Vernon Presley and Dee Stanley (holding hands) in 1960.

★ SURRENDER SLOW-COOKED MUSTARD GREENS ★

4 **pounds mustard greens, or collard, kale, turnip, or beet tops**

1 **large onion, chopped**

1 **4-ounce slab salt pork, cubed**
Pepper
Red wine vinegar
Hot pepper sauce

Discard the stems and soak the greens to remove the dirt. In a deep skillet sauté the onion in the pork cubes (to render pork cubes, add water to cubes and steam uncovered until the water evaporates and the fat fries out).

In a stock pot blanch the greens in boiling water for 10 minutes. Drain. Stir the greens into the onion. Add pepper to taste. Cover and cook on low heat for 45 minutes. Dish up and add a little red wine vinegar and hot pepper sauce.

Serves 6.

Lucille Luongo
Elvis fan and Past National President,
American Women in Radio and Television
New York, New York

Aunt Delta and her beloved dog Edmund I take a look
at some of Elvis's many stage costumes.

*TENNESSEE TUXEDO?—This 1956 photo shows Elvis
looking mighty formal for a TV special.*

★ YOUNG LOVE FRIED OKRA ★

1	**quart young okra**
2	**quarts boiling water**
2	**teaspoons salt**
2	**cups yellow cornmeal**
2	**cups cooking oil**
	Salt and pepper

Wash the okra, discard the stems, and cut into ¼-inch pieces. Parboil in 2 quarts of salted boiling water for 5 to 7 minutes. Drain in a colander. Sprinkle with salt and pepper and roll in cornmeal. Let rest for 20 to 30 minutes so the cornmeal will stick to the okra when you are ready to begin frying. Fry in deep oil just a few minutes or until golden. Drain on paper towels and season immediately with salt and pepper. **Serves 4.**

Jean Busby
Elvis Country Fan Club

★ COUNTRY COOKED OKRA ★ (BOILED OR FRIED)

For Boiled:

1	**pound okra**
1	**teaspoon salt**
	Margarine
1	**tablespoon lemon juice**

For Fried:

1	**pound okra**
1	**cup all-purpose flour**
	Vegetable oil
	Salt

For boiled: Use fresh okra! Wash and remove the stems. If boiling, be careful not to cut into the pod or the okra will become slimy. Place the okra and salt in a saucepan. Cover with water and cook over medium heat for about 10 minutes. Drain and serve with melted margarine to taste and lemon juice.

For fried: Wash the okra and remove the stems. Cut into ½-inch pieces and place in a bowl. Sprinkle a small amount of water over the okra, so it will be damp but not wet. Sift the flour over the okra while you are waiting to cook it.

In a frying pan heat enough oil to cover the bottom over high heat. Reduce the heat to medium high. Sift the okra through your fingers onto the plate. Rake the okra into the frying pan. Be sure not to crowd the okra in the frying pan to make sure they will get brown but not mushy. Let the okra start to brown before stirring so the flour will not come off the okra. With a slotted spoon or spatula, remove the okra when brown and drain in a colander. Repeat until all of the okra is fried. Sprinkle salt over the okra while hot. **Serves 6.**

Betty Jo McMichael
Co-owner, Whistle Stop Cafe
Irondale, Alabama

★ SQUASH CASSEROLE DELUXE ★

1½ **pounds squash, sliced and cooked**
1 **medium onion, chopped**
2 **cups water**
1 **teaspoon salt**
 Dash pepper
3 **tablespoons butter**
1 **cup grated sharp Cheddar cheese**
2 **eggs, separated**
10 **crackers, crumbled**

Preheat the oven to 350°. In a large bowl mix all of the ingredients together except for the egg whites. Beat the egg whites stiff and fold into the mixture. Pour into a casserole dish. Bake about 30 minutes until done.

Serves 4 to 6.

Laverne Whitman
Tampa, Florida

★ SUMMERTIME SQUASH CASSEROLE ★

8 **or 9 small squash, sliced**
1 **10¾-ounce can cream of mushroom soup**
1 **cup grated cheese**
1 **cup chopped onion**
 Crackers, crushed
¼ **cup (½ stick) margarine**

Preheat the oven to 350°. In a large mixing bowl combine the squash, soup, cheese, and onion. Pour into a baking dish. Top with crushed buttery crackers. Drizzle melted margarine over the top. Bake for 30 minutes.

Serves 4 to 5.

Marie Isbell
Sylacauga, Alabama

Elvis finding time for a quick snack.

★ HOOSIER BAKED SQUASH ★

2	pounds zucchini or yellow summer squash
3	tablespoons chopped onion
3	eggs, beaten
½	teaspoon hot pepper sauce
2	teaspoons chopped parsley
	Salt and pepper to taste
½	cup (1 stick) butter, melted
2	cups cracker crumbs

Preheat the oven to 350°. Slice the squash into ½-inch pieces. Boil 3 minutes or until tender. Drain. Add the onion, eggs, and seasonings, and mix until well blended. Pour into a 1-quart casserole dish. Mix the butter and crumbs, and sprinkle over the squash. Bake for 35 to 40 minutes.

Serves 6.

Varnice Hacker Humphries
Cousin of Elvis Presley

Everybody was rockin' when Elvis took the stage with (left to right) Scotty Moore, D. J. Fontana, and Bill Black (hidden behind Elvis).

★ FRAN'S ZUCCHINI SAUTÉ ★

4   **to 6 zucchini, thinly sliced**
2   **tablespoons margarine**
2   **tablespoons olive oil**
    Fresh black pepper to taste
1   **medium yellow onion, finely diced
    (optional)**
2   **cloves garlic, minced (optional)**
⅓   **cup grated Parmesan (or Cheddar)
    cheese**
    Sliced mushrooms (optional)

Arrange the zucchini slices on paper towels and set aside for about 30 minutes to drain. In a skillet heat the margarine, olive oil, and pepper, and sauté the squash over medium heat. Add the onion and garlic, if desired. When the squash becomes a little translucent but still firm, add the grated cheese, and then toss for 2 to 3 minutes.

The zucchini will shrink a little during cooking. I recommend that you prepare 2 zucchini per person if you really like them. Sliced mushrooms can also be added.

Serves 3 or 4.

Francine and Cecil Blackwood
The Blackwood Brothers

ELVIS AND PRISCILLA PRESLEY'S MARRIAGE WAS A SURPRISE EVENT. THEY TOOK A FEW FRIENDS AND FAMILY MEMBERS AND FLEW IN THE MIDDLE OF THE NIGHT FROM PALM SPRINGS, WHERE ELVIS WAS SHOOTING *CLAMBAKE*, TO LAS VEGAS. THEY GOT IN AT 3 A.M. AND BY 3:30 A.M. THEY HAD THEIR MARRIAGE LICENSE. THE TWO WERE MARRIED THE FOLLOWING MORNING AT 9:41 A.M. (MAY 1, 1967) IN A DOUBLE RING CEREMONY AT THE ALADDIN HOTEL. AFTER THE WEDDING, THERE WAS A PRESS CONFERENCE. THE JUBILANT COUPLE RETURNED TO PALM SPRINGS THAT NIGHT AND ELVIS RESUMED WORK ON HIS MOVIE. THE COUPLE DID NOT CELEBRATE THEIR HONEYMOON UNTIL AFTER THE MOVIE WRAPPED. THEN THE TWO WENT TO ELVIS'S CIRCLE G RANCH IN WALLS, MISS., WHERE THERE WAS A BEAUTIFUL HOME ON THE RANCH BUT THERE WAS ALSO A TRAILER. THE BRIDE AND GROOM STAYED IN THE TRAILER RATHER THAN THE HOUSE BECAUSE ELVIS THOUGHT IT WOULD BE A GREAT EXPERIENCE TO LIVE IN A MOBILE HOME.

★ Stuffed Zucchini Fellini ★

	Salt and pepper
4	**zucchini halves**
½	**small onion, chopped**
3½	**slices white bread or Italian bread-crumbs**
2	**eggs, beaten**
¼	**cup grated Parmesan cheese**
¼	**cup shredded Cheddar cheese**
	Butter

Preheat the oven to 350°. Salt and pepper the zucchinis to taste. In a large pot boil them in salted water for about 5 minutes. Scoop out the middle of the zucchini halves and dice. In a medium bowl combine the diced zucchini, onion, bread, eggs, Parmesan, and Cheddar. Stir well and stuff into the zucchini shells. Dot the shells with butter, place in a baking pan, and bake for 20 to 30 minutes.

Serves 4.

Sue Hardesty
Cousin of Elvis Presley

Elvis has a ball on the set of Follow That Dream *with fellow cast members, twins Pam and Pat Ogles.*

★ BIKINI ZUCCHINI CASSEROLE ★

4   pounds medium-sized zucchini
1   pound bulk pork sausage
½   cup chopped onion
28 saltine crackers, crushed
4   eggs, slightly beaten
    Salt and pepper to taste
½   teaspoon thyme
2   garlic cloves, pressed
1   cup grated Parmesan cheese

Preheat the oven to 350°. Wash the zucchini and trim the ends. In a large pot of boiling, salted water cook the zucchini for 12 to 15 minutes or until almost tender. Drain and chop coarsely. Cook the sausage and onion until the sausage browns. Drain off the grease. In a large bowl combine the zucchini, sausage, and remaining ingredients, except for ¼ cup of the cheese. Spoon into a 3-quart casserole, and sprinkle the cheese on top. Bake for 60 to 70 minutes, until bubbly.

You can make this ahead, refrigerate, remove for 1 hour, and then bake.

Serves 8.

Jessica Mitchell
Cobourg, Ontario

SMILES ABOUT ELVIS—Remembering Elvis are (clockwise from top left) Edie Hand, Donna Presley Early, Graceland liaison Patsy Anderson, and one of Elvis's personal nurses, Marian Cocke.

★ ANYPLACE IS PARADISE ★ ASPARAGUS CASSEROLE

1	16-ounce can asparagus spears, drained
1	16-ounce can green peas, drained
1	7-ounce can sliced water chestnuts, drained
1	to 2 10¾-ounce cans cream of mushroom soup
1	cup breadcrumbs
4	slices processed cheese
1	6-ounce can sliced mushrooms (optional)

Preheat the oven to 350°. Layer half of the asparagus, peas, water chestnuts, and soup in a baking dish. Repeat the layers. Top with breadcrumbs. Bake for 20 to 25 minutes or until bubbly.

Top with the cheese and bake until the cheese melts. If desired, you can add sliced mushrooms to the mixture.

Serves 6 to 8.

Mary Whitney
Tulsa, Oklahoma

LISA MARIE LOVED FRENCH FRIES. THE COOKS WOULD FIX HER UP A BIG DISH OF THEM. SHE WOULD COME OUT TO THE OFFICE WHERE COUSINS PATSY AND DONNA WERE WORKING AND SIT AND TALK ABOUT SCHOOL, BOYS, AND WHATEVER ELSE WAS GOING ON IN HER LIFE. SHE ONCE TOLD DONNA THAT MICHAEL JACKSON WAS HER FAVORITE PERFORMER.

This early family portrait shows a very young Elvis with his mother, Gladys, and father, Vernon.
Elvis's lip twitch is one of his most famous trademark poses, but in truth it began as a result of a bribe.
While they were posing for this portrait, Elvis wouldn't quit talking. So his parents bribed him with a peanut.
He has it in his mouth, and thus the famous twitch was born.

MAKING GREAT STRIDES—Elvis was already going places in 1956.
He always had a car nearby.

★ RUSTY'S BROCCOLI CASSEROLE ★

2   10-ounce packages frozen broccoli, chopped
1   10¾-ounce can cream of mushroom soup
1   cup mayonnaise
    Salt and pepper to taste
1   small onion, chopped
1   cup grated Cheddar cheese
½   cup (1 stick) butter, melted
1   14-ounce package herb stuffing mix

Preheat the oven to 350°. Cook the broccoli according to the package directions. Drain and place in a casserole dish. Mix in the soup, mayonnaise, salt and pepper, and onion. Sprinkle with cheese. Mix the butter and stuffing mix and sprinkle over the top. Bake for 45 minutes.
Serves 6.

Karen Brackett
Atlanta, Georgia

★ CAN DO CORN AND BEAN CASSEROLE ★

1   16-ounce can white shoe peg corn, drained
1   16-ounce can French cut green beans, drained
½   cup chopped onion
½   cup sour cream
1   cup grated Cheddar cheese
1   10¾-ounce can cream of celery soup

Topping:
24   rich buttery crackers, crushed
1½   cups (3 sticks) margarine, melted
¾   cup chopped almonds

Preheat the oven to 350°. In a 1½-quart casserole dish combine the corn, green beans, onion, sour cream, Cheddar cheese, and soup.

In a medium bowl combine the crackers, margarine, and almonds. Pour over the casserole and bake for 30 to 35 minutes.
Serves 4 to 6.

Rachel Baldwin
Tampa, Florida

★ FAIR IS MOVING ON CORN CASSEROLE ★

2	tablespoons butter
½	cup chopped onion
¼	cup chopped bell pepper
¼	cup chopped celery
1	15-ounce can whole corn
1	15-ounce can creamed corn
2	eggs
1	cup milk
¼	cup grated cheese
1	cup cracker crumbs

Preheat the oven to 350°. In a skillet melt the butter and sauté the onion, bell pepper, and celery. In a casserole dish combine the sautéed mixture and remaining ingredients. Bake for 55 minutes.

Serves 6.

Verna Melohn
Elvis fan

THE UNITED STATES POSTAL SYSTEM UNVEILED ITS ELVIS STAMP AT GRACELAND ON JANUARY 8, 1993, BUT DUE TO AN ERROR, THE ACTUAL FIRST DAY OF ISSUE STAMPS OCCURRED IN LATE DECEMBER IN AMARILLO, TEXAS. THE POSTAL SERVICE MISTAKENLY SHIPPED SOME OF THE STAMPS TO THE AMARILLO POST OFFICE ABOUT TWELVE DAYS BEFORE THEY WERE TO BE OFFICIALLY RELEASED. SO THE AMARILLO POST OFFICE SOLD ITS ELVIS STAMPS SEVERAL DAYS BEFORE THE OFFICIAL PREMIERE OF THE STAMPS.

★ PUT THE BLAME ON ME CORN PUDDING ★

1 15-ounce can whole corn
1 15-ounce can creamed corn
2 or 3 tablespoons sugar
½ to 1 cup milk
1 teaspoon vanilla extract
2 or 3 tablespoons all-purpose flour
1 or 2 eggs

Preheat the oven to 350°. In a casserole dish combine all of the ingredients. Bake for 1 hour and 30 minutes to 2 hours or until a knife inserted in the center comes out clean.

Serves 6.

Shirley Beattie
Presley-Ites Fan Club
Orlando, Florida

Rock 'n' roll!

Elvis in concert in 1968.

★ SWEETHEART SWEET POTATO SURPRISE ★

10   **medium-sized sweet potatoes**
2   **tablespoons vegetable oil**
¾   **cup butter or margarine**
⅓   **cup bourbon**
½   **teaspoon salt**
½   **cup coarsely chopped walnuts or**
        pecans
2   **tablespoons butter or margarine**

Preheat the oven to 350°. Wash the sweet potatoes well. Rub them with vegetable oil. Place the potatoes on a baking sheet and bake for 1 hour or until tender. Cool the potatoes to the touch. Remove the pulp.

In a large bowl combine the pulp, butter or margarine, bourbon, and salt. Beat with an electric mixer until light and fluffy. Stir in the nuts, reserving 2 tablespoons for garnish. Spoon the potato mixture into a lightly greased 1-quart casserole. Dot with butter and sprinkle with the reserved nuts. Bake for 20 minutes.

Serves 8.

Jackie Hacker Coleman
Cousin of Elvis Presley

CHRISTMAS AT GRACELAND WAS ALWAYS VERY SPECIAL. THE MANSION WAS ALWAYS DECORATED FOR THE HOLIDAYS, AND NASH'S HUSBAND, EARL, AND A COWORKER WOULD DRIVE TO MISSISSIPPI AND GET A LARGE, LIVE TREE FOR THE DINING ROOM. ON CHRISTMAS EVE EVERYONE WOULD GATHER AROUND THE DINING ROOM TABLE TO EXCHANGE GIFTS. ELVIS WOULD BUY GIFT CERTIFICATES AT GOLDSMITH'S DEPARTMENT STORE AND PASS THEM OUT.

Lunch time, Sheffield, Alabama. Elvis waits his turn for a double order of Southern fried chicken, milk, and snowball cakes before getting back on the train to continue his trip to Memphis, Tennessee. The date, July 4, 1956.

★ HARD KNOCKS HASH BROWNS ★

1	pound thick-sliced bacon, cut into ½-inch pieces
1	26-ounce bag frozen hash browns
1	green bell pepper, chopped
1	to 3 hot pepper pods (to taste), chopped
1	large onion, chopped
2	4-ounce cans mushroom halves, drained (optional)
6	eggs

In a large nonstick skillet fry the bacon. Cook the potatoes in the bacon drippings for 5 minutes, stirring frequently and being careful not to let the potatoes stick. Transfer the potatoes to a microwave-safe container and cook in the microwave oven for 10 minutes.

Meanwhile, stir the peppers, onions, and mushrooms in the bacon drippings. Cook and stir for 2 minutes. Return the potatoes to the skillet and add the eggs. Cook and stir until the eggs are scrambled.

Serves 4.

Sandi and Willie Wynn

Elvis the heartthrob.

★ PROUD MARY POCATELLO POTATOES ★

1	cup (2 sticks) margarine, melted
½	cup chopped onions
1	10¾-ounce can cream of mushroom soup
7	or 8 potatoes, boiled in their jackets, sliced
1	pound processed cheese, cubed
½	cup chopped onions
1	4-ounce jar pimientos
1	cup breadcrumbs
½	teaspoon onion salt
½	teaspoon garlic salt
2	tablespoons chopped parsley

Topping:
¼	cup shredded Cheddar cheese
½	teaspoon paprika

Preheat the oven to 350°. In a skillet melt the margarine and cook the onions with the mushroom soup. Transfer to a casserole dish and add the remaining ingredients. Stir well. Sprinkle with cheese and paprika. Bake for 30 minutes or until the cheese is melted and browned.
Serves 6 to 8.

Wanda Sprung
Tampa, Florida

★ DELECTABLE SWEET POTATOES ★

6	medium sweet potatoes
¼	cup (½ stick) butter, melted
1	teaspoon salt
2	tablespoons pineapple juice
1¼	cups crushed pineapple, drained
10	marshmallows, quartered

Preheat the oven to 400°. Bake the potatoes for 35 minutes. Scoop out the pulp. In a large bowl whip the potatoes with the melted butter, salt, and pineapple juice until fluffy. Stir in the crushed pineapple. Transfer to a greased 6 x 10-inch baking dish and top with marshmallows. Bake for 15 to 20 minutes.
Serves 8.

Michelle Johnston
Chattanooga, Tennessee

★ CRUNCHY SWEET POTATO CASSEROLE ★

3	cups mashed, cooked sweet potatoes
1	cup sugar
2	eggs
½	cup evaporated milk
½	cup (1 stick) butter, melted
1	teaspoon vanilla extract
1	cup firmly packed brown sugar
⅓	cup all-purpose flour
⅓	cup butter, melted
½	to 1 cup chopped pecans

Preheat the oven to 350°. In a large bowl combine the sweet potatoes, sugar, eggs, evaporated milk, ½ cup of butter, and vanilla. Mix well and spoon into a baking dish. In a small dish combine the brown sugar, flour, ⅓ cup of butter, and pecans. Sprinkle over the sweet potato mixture. Bake for 30 minutes.

Serves 8.

Betty Jo McMichael
Co-owner, Whistle Stop Cafe
Irondale, Alabama

SOMETIMES ELVIS WOULD GIVE OUT GIFT
CERTIFICATES FROM A LOCAL FAST-FOOD
RESTAURANT AS A JOKE BEFORE HE GAVE OUT
HIS REAL CHRISTMAS GIFTS.

★ SWEET CAROLINE SWEET POTATO CASSEROLE ★

3	cups cooked sweet potatoes
2	large eggs, slightly beaten
1	cup sugar
1½	teaspoons vanilla extract
1	cup frozen coconut
½	cup (1 stick) butter

Topping:

1	cup chopped walnuts
½	cup (1 stick) butter
1	cup firmly packed brown sugar
½	cup self-rising flour

Preheat the oven to 350°. In a large bowl mix together the potatoes, eggs, sugar, vanilla, coconut, and butter. Pour into a large casserole dish and bake for 20 minutes.

While baking, in a large bowl combine the walnuts, ½ cup of butter, brown sugar, and flour. Remove the casserole from the oven when done and drizzle the topping mixture over it. Return the casserole to the oven and bake until the topping is brown. Be careful not to overbake, because the topping will be tough.

Serves 6.

Marie Isbell
Sylacauga, Alabama

★ CRUSTY POTATO PANCAKES ★

2	pounds potatoes
¼	cup grated white onion
3	eggs
¾	cup all-purpose flour
2	teaspoons salt
	Oil for frying
1	23-ounce jar applesauce

Peel and coarsely grate the potatoes into a bowl of cold water. (This keeps them from turning dark and removes the excess starch.) In a separate bowl make a batter by mixing the onion, eggs, flour, and salt. Drain the potatoes, pressing out all of the liquid. Beat the potatoes into the batter. Heat the oil in a skillet or on a griddle. Spoon the heaping teaspoons of batter into the skillet, spreading the batter with the back of the spoon into 4-inch rounds. Brown on one side, turn, and brown on the other side. Brown the pancakes slowly so the potatoes will cook through properly. Drain on absorbent paper. Serve warm with the applesauce.

Serves 6.

Debbie Busby
Elvis Country Fan Club

Elvis at his performing best.

★ HEART OF ROME GARLIC MASHED POTATOES ★ WITH FRIZZLED ONIONS

4	medium garlic cloves, peeled
½	teaspoon olive oil
8	small russet potatoes
½	cup milk
6	tablespoons (¾ stick) butter
2	ounces cream cheese
	Salt and pepper to taste
½	cup sour cream, room temperature

Frizzled Onions:

2	tablespoons all-purpose flour
	Salt and pepper
	Pinch paprika
	Pinch cayenne
1	medium white onion, thinly sliced
½	cup canola oil

Preheat the oven to 450°. Place the garlic cloves on a 6-inch square piece of aluminum foil. Drizzle with the olive oil. Close the foil and roast for 30 minutes.

Bake the potatoes in the oven until soft. Then mash the potatoes. Set aside. Remove the garlic from the foil. Cut off the top of each clove and squeeze the garlic paste into a saucepan. Add the milk, butter, cream cheese, and salt and pepper to the garlic. Heat and stir until smooth. Blend in the mashed potatoes, and add the sour cream.

To make frizzled onions, in a bowl whisk together the flour, salt and pepper, paprika, and cayenne. Toss the onion slices in the flour, mix together well, and shake off the excess batter from the onions. In a skillet heat the canola oil and fry the onions. Drain on paper.

Serves 6.

Clyniece Blackburn Ledbetter
Red Bay, Alabama

ELVIS LOVED CHRISTMAS. IT WAS
HIS FAVORITE TIME OF YEAR.

Graceland: Yesteryear and Today

by Donna Presley Early

My mother, Nash Lorene Presley Pritchett, was the younger sister to Elvis's father, Vernon, and uncle Vester. Thus, Elvis and I were first cousins, although I was fifteen years younger than Elvis.

I was born and grew up in East Prairie, Missouri, which is about a two-and-a-half hour drive from Graceland in Memphis. Elvis bought the mansion for $100,000 from a Dr. Thomas Moore, who had built the house in 1939 and named it after his aunt Grace. Elvis moved into the place with his mother, Gladys, and father, Vernon, in the spring of 1957 when he was twenty-two.

My first trip to Graceland came in the fall of 1958 with my parents and sister when I was eight. My first impression was that it was huge. And with 17,552 square feet, it is big—even by today's standards.

"What a mansion," I thought. It was so beautiful. The house is built of stone in a traditional Southern Colonial style. Everything was so flamboyant. Elvis liked simple things but he also liked that flair that set him apart from everybody else, and that included his home.

The front drive and lawn of Graceland in the spring.

When he came back from the service in Germany, my mom and sister and I came down from Missouri. I was ten at the time. Normally family and friends came around to the back of the house, but for some reason the cab driver brought us to the front, up the long driveway. Elvis opened the door. He was dressed in black. How handsome he was. He hugged and kissed all of us, and this is

one of my earliest and most vivid memories of coming to Graceland.

Today, that front driveway is used by the tour buses shuttling the thousands of tourists who come daily to see the house that was home sweet home to Elvis Presley. More than seven hundred thousand fans annually make the rock 'n' roll pilgrimage to Graceland. Tourists park in a huge lot, walk a couple of hundred yards to the enclosed ticketing offices, and then hop on a bus that simply crosses the street, aptly named Elvis Presley Boulevard, and scoots on up the driveway. It's probably less than a city block, maybe three hundred yards, and you'd think the fans could just walk it, but the buses help keep things flowing smoothly.

Earl Pritchett is in perfect harmony in front of the famous gates of Graceland.

The front lawn of Graceland is huge with lots of tall trees. The estate sits on nearly fourteen acres of green grass and rolling hills. A brick wall acts as a barrier between the yard and Elvis Presley Boulevard. The famous white iron gates are still in place with their black musical notes.

Near the front of the house are white, ornamental lions guarding the steps that lead up to the front door. When I was younger Elvis used to have several pink flamingos perched nearby as well.

When I turned ten, Elvis asked my parents if I could stay permanently at Graceland, to keep company with my grandma who lived there, and he promised them that he would take good care of me. My parents didn't think that was such a hot idea, but they did agree to let me spend my summers there. So from age ten throughout my teenage years, I would pack my things and go to Graceland for the summer months. It was terrific.

My grandmother and I were very close. I spent most of my time with her. We watched TV. She loved Westerns. I read to her. We listened to music, and we danced. Elvis had lots of pets, including chickens. So every day, Grandma and I would go out and gather the eggs. The people who worked there treated me like a queen.

At this time in the early 1960s, there were probably about ten employees on the estate. There was a guard at the gate and there were several lawn-maintenance people. There were almost always two cooks, who essentially doubled as maids in the house, two in the day and two at night. And there were two secretaries in Vernon's office out back. One of them was Patsy, my uncle Vester's daughter. She was my first cousin, my confidant, and also one of my best friends.

In those days, Elvis sometimes would allow the security guards to open the gates so the fans could walk up to the front of the house for a closer look. When Elvis was not at home, I loved nothing better than to go outside and talk and visit with the people.

There is a huge tree in the front yard, on the right if you're facing Graceland, and I would go out there with a picnic lunch and sit on the top of the hill and watch people standing outside the gate. One of my favorite desserts was tapioca pudding. Daisy, one of the cooks, would always fix this for me in a little pudding dish. In fact, she would fix all of my lunch, and I would sit under the tree and eat nonchalantly, while I'm sure the people were wondering who I was and why I should be allowed to picnic on Elvis's front lawn.

Some days I would walk down to the front gate and talk to the fans. They were very interested in Graceland because of their love for Elvis. I got to meet people from all over the world. Often they couldn't speak English and I couldn't speak their language. But we were always able to communicate because, I guess, "Elvis" was a universal language. One morning I communicated with a French girl who couldn't speak English but she could write it. So we communicated for an hour or so, just sitting there writing notes back and forth.

If you take the Graceland tour today, you'll enter the house by the front door. The living room will be the first room on your right. It's decorated in classic '60s motif and is the most formal room in the house. It was redecorated in the 1970s and features stained-glass peacocks, a long, white couch, white carpet, and a fireplace.

As hard as it may be to believe today, there were occasions when Elvis would call down to the front and invite a few fans to come up to the house and sit in the living room for a few minutes. Elvis was really very warm and enjoyed meeting people. He knew that he once had their same aspirations and dreams, and he never forgot about that. He believed we were all the same.

On the far side of the living room is Elvis's music room with his black baby grand piano and TV set. I used to watch a lot of television in the music room with Jean Boyd, a close family friend. I remember one time, real late at night, when Jean and I were watching "Sivad," the host of a local Memphis TV station's horror movie show. There was a lot of wind outside and it was raining. At the most dramatic moment in the film the branches of the trees and bushes outside of the music room scraped loudly against the window, and it scared us to death. We ran screaming from the music room to Grandma's bedroom for refuge.

I remember Elvis playing the piano, and he and his friends would sing. This was an especially favorite place at Christmas time, as we would all sing Christmas carols. A lot of parties were held in the living room and music room.

Christmas at Graceland in 1992. Left to right are Susie Pritchett, Donna Presley Early, their mother (Elvis's aunt) Nash Presley Pritchett, and Aunt Delta.

In the entry way and living room was where Elvis performed a lot of karate exhibitions, entertaining his friends. He really got a kick out of that. There is a crystal chandelier above the entryway.

The dining room is to the left as you enter Graceland. This room was always very warm and cheerful. At Christmas time the tree was always put up in here. Everybody would sit around and talk.

There is another gorgeous chandelier over the dining room table, and candles are always on the table. (The previous chandelier was very unusual and had large leaves hanging down.) The dining room has a beautiful black marble floor. We had family dinners there, even when Elvis was gone (out touring or making movies), with Uncle Vernon, Grandma, Dee (Vernon's wife at the time), Aunt Delta, Mama, and Daddy, and my sister and me. In the summers, when it was just Grandma and me, most of the time we ate in the kitchen.

From the dining room you can enter the kitchen, which was the focal point of Graceland. Everybody would meet in the kitchen. Most of the time Elvis would eat breakfast in the kitchen (this would be in the late afternoon since he was a night owl). Grandma and I always ate breakfast and lunch in the kitchen. Here I enjoyed chatting away with the cooks. Elvis also loved to sit around the kitchen. It was filled with a lot of warmth and joy, not to mention good ol' Southern cooking, with the lot of us (family, friends, and employees) talking and laughing like one big, happy family. There were a number of cooks over the years, and I fondly remember Daisy, Lottie, Nancy, Pauline, and Mary.

Near the kitchen you can go down a mirrored staircase to the basement of Graceland, where, to your left, you will enter the bright yellow and navy blue TV room. Elvis had three TV sets lined up horizontally here, so he could watch several football games at the same time. (Two of Elvis's favorite teams were the Cleveland Browns and Pittsburgh Steelers.) But the room was designed for entertainment of all kinds. Above the TV sets is a pull-down movie screen. The room also has a record player and stereo system. There is a blue couch designed in a giant U-shape and it is loaded with white and yellow pillows that sparkle with glitter. There is a mirrored soda fountain, upholstered in yellow vinyl, directly to your right as you go into the TV room. The room was decorated in its current manner in 1974.

The TV Room.

We used to spend a lot of time there because Elvis enjoyed movies, and the family and friends would go down to the basement and watch TV. Elvis loved to narrate what was going on and he would tell you what was going to happen next. He loved animal shows like *Wild Kingdom* and those life-and-death matches between lions and boa constrictors, and that sort of thing. I remember he really was a big fan of *I Love Lucy,* and, as for movie stars, he really enjoyed Spencer Tracy and Katharine Hepburn.

Elvis was really in awe of many actors. His two favorite films of his own were *Love Me Tender* and *King Creole.* He always wanted to be a serious dramatic actor, and thus people who succeeded in this impressed him.

I played a lot down there in the TV room and watched a lot of TV with Priscilla. I always enjoyed the soda fountain with its icy, sweet treats of ice cream and milk shakes and floats. I guess the thing that impressed me most was that he had his own projector and would run these films. Back in my small town we all had to go to a theater, but Elvis had a movie theater in his own home. That was pretty awesome in the early 1960s.

Across from the TV room is Elvis's pool room. Elvis and the guys would go down there a lot and shoot pool and sit around and talk. It seemed very luxurious to me with its walls lined with pleated fabric imported from England in a variety of colors. (Elvis picked out the motif from a magazine.) He was a good pool player. He wanted to be good at everything he did.

From the pool room the Graceland tour takes you into the famous "Jungle Room." When I was a young girl, there was no Jungle Room. This was a screened-in porch with furniture and a record player, and a place where I could sit and listen to music.

The famous Jungle Room, around 1975.

The Jungle Room all started as a joke. Elvis was at a furniture store, and Uncle Vernon wondered out loud, "Who in the world would buy this?"

The next day Elvis had it delivered to Graceland.

The Jungle Room did become a favorite of Elvis. With its green shag carpeting and the wild and woolly decor, among other things, it reminded him of Hawaii, which was his favorite vacation spot. I loved it, too, and I had never been to Hawaii. The stone waterfall was so beautiful with its colored lights, and the water was always running. When he decided to record his *From Elvis Presley Boulevard* album in there was when he had the carpet put on

all the walls. I remember them bringing in all the recording equipment and the drums and microphones. This was also where we would watch out in the back yard on the Fourth of July and Christmas, when Elvis and the guys would set off fireworks and shoot Roman candles at one another.

The upstairs of Graceland is not on the tour, but I'll share a few quick memories of what was up there.

Dodger Presley visits with son Vernon in her room at Graceland.

Grandma's bedroom was upstairs in the early years. She had a gigantic bed. When I was a girl, many times I would share the bed with Grandma, and later, after Elvis married Priscilla, there were nights when Elvis was away on tour, that I would sleep on one side of Grandma and Priscilla would sleep on the other side. Later, Grandma's bedroom became Lisa Marie's room. There also was a guest room upstairs, which later became Elvis's closet.

And there was Elvis's apartment. You entered between two padded, golden doors. He had a living area/conference room combined. To the left of this room was a ladies' bathroom and to the right was his bedroom and bathroom. The conference room had orange, shag carpet and gold, leather-padded walls with white buttons and iridescent, purple draperies. I know that sounds terrible but it was a beautiful combination. I actually spent the night one

This is the stairway that leads to Elvis's bedroom at Graceland.

The Bible and pearl necklace of Grandmother Minnie Mae "Dodger" Presley rest on the bedside table in her room at Graceland.

time sleeping on a pallet on the conference room floor. Well, enough about the upstairs.

When you exit the back door and the Jungle Room, you'll walk past the carport and notice Lisa Marie's swing set in the back yard. Then you'll see Vernon Presley's office. When I was a little girl I spent a lot of time in there visiting with my cousin Patsy and the other secretaries, like Pat Boyd. On January 3, 1979, I started working for Vernon in that office. My main job was to answer fan mail. I did this until 1982. By then the atmosphere at Graceland had changed. It had gone from being totally family oriented to a lot of strangers.

This is the view of the back of Graceland as seen from Vernon Presley's office. This is the entrance that was used by the Presley family.

Don't misunderstand me. I'm glad they opened it for the fans. I think Elvis would love it that his loyal followers are now able to see where he lived and the family environment along with all of his

accolades, but at the time it really became hard for me because of my own personal family affections.

The back yard of Graceland was spacious. It was here where Elvis often quarterbacked touch football games, shot off fireworks, and rode horses. Elvis loved to ride horses. He had a palomino named Rising Sun, and a stable with about fourteen horses. He didn't like to do anything alone, so if he did something, he made sure others could do

Vernon and Dee Presley's house on Dolan Drive was on property just behind Graceland.

it too. That included riding horses, go-carts, motorcycles, and golf carts. They go-carted on the front drive and they drove golf carts in the back. Many times Elvis liked to get away by himself, so he would get in a golf cart and just drive around the grounds.

Lisa Marie had her own golf cart, which she loved and would ride around all over the place. My sons would ride with her too. She only knew one speed: wide open, just like her dad. The cart had Lisa Marie's name painted on its side.

Lisa Marie and a friend pause for a picture during a journey around Graceland in Lisa Marie's golf cart.

In 1969, my mom, dad, sister, and I moved to the back of Graceland into the mobile home that Elvis had bought for himself and Priscilla for their honeymoon. My dad became supervisor over maintenance. My parents lived there until about 1986. I lived there until 1971, but came back to visit often and my two sons spent a lot of time at Graceland visiting their grandparents.

From the back yard the Graceland tour will take you back into the house to the Trophy Room. This used to be a patio years back with a jukebox and lots of tables and chairs to sit in beside the swimming pool. When Elvis decided to close it in, he made it into a slot-car room with a huge track for racing slot cars.

The Trophy Room is home of many of Elvis's elaborate costumes and awards of all types.

Now it is filled with lots of memorabilia from his phenomenal career. You can see photographs from his early television appearances, his famous 1957 gold lamé outfit, posters from many of his movies, giant, oversized photographs, and the clothes he and Priscilla wore when they got married in 1967. From the Trophy Room, you will walk down the eighty-foot Hall of Gold, which is filled with his many gold records from the United States and around the world.

Also on display is a myriad of personal mementos, ranging from his Army uniform and boxing warm-up robe from *Kid Galahad* to many of the gorgeous costumes from his films and concert appearances and TV specials. There are scrapbooks from his fans, the gold belt for his record-breaking Las Vegas engagements, some of his guitars, paintings of Elvis, tour costumes, his Eagle cape, karate

uniforms, jumpsuits, and even his gun and badge collections.

Going back outside you can walk over to Elvis's racquetball room. Here he had a pinball machine, an incline board for sit-ups, a lounge area, and the racquetball court itself, now with its walls filled to the gills with album and record artwork. He had a sauna upstairs and on the top was a walking track.

Finally, you'll see Meditation Garden. Elvis had that built as a place of relaxing and enjoyment, never knowing it would become his final resting place.

Earl Pritchett stands guard over one of the many fine cars that were part of the rolling stock at Graceland.

The garden has a pool with six spewing fountains. There are two holly trees, some benches, and a twelve-foot-high statue of Jesus with two angels.

Here fans solemnly take in the graves of Elvis, his mother, Gladys, daddy, Vernon, and grandmother Minnie Mae from a curving brick wall, decorated with stained-glass windows and a semicircle of eight Greek-inspired pillars. An enclosed flame burns at the head of Elvis's grave. Multitudes of fans from around the globe leave their floral tributes and messages here.

I go about once a year to Meditation Garden, usually on the anniversary of his death. There was a time when it was very hard for me to go here, but now I find it is a good place to think back and remember the good times I spent with Elvis and my family and friends at Graceland.

GRACELAND INFORMATION

Graceland is located approximately 10 miles from downtown Memphis and only a few minutes from the Memphis International Airport. From Interstate 55 take Exit 5-B (Elvis Presley Boulevard) approximately one mile south to Graceland. The parking lot is located on the west side of Elvis Presley Boulevard, across the street from Graceland mansion.

Graceland is open daily Memorial Day through Labor Day from 8 A.M. to 6 P.M. The remainder of the year it is open 9 A.M. to 5 P.M. Tours of Graceland are not available on Tuesdays from November through February. It is closed New Year's Day, Thanksgiving Day, and Christmas Day.

Admission for the Graceland tour is $10 for adults, $9 for senior citizens, and $5 for children ages 7 to 12.

For reservations, call 1-800-238-2000.

Buddy Early, a Graceland security guard and husband of Donna Presley Early, places a floral arrangement on Elvis's grave in 1980 as Graceland visitors pay their respects.

EVERY FAN'S DREAM—The stub from an admission ticket to Graceland.

★ FRANKFORT SPECIAL LOW-FAT BAKED BEANS ★

1   **16-ounce can pork and beans**
2   **tablespoons firmly packed dark brown sugar**
1   **small onion, chopped**
2   **tablespoons ketchup**
¼   **teaspoon mustard**

Preheat the oven to 350°. In a medium bowl combine all of the ingredients. Mix well. Pour into a baking dish. Bake for 25 minutes. **Serves 4 to 6.**

Michelle Elaine
President, TCM for Elvis Fan Club
Chicago, Illinois

Composers Mike Stoller (left) and Jerry Leiber look over some music with Elvis on MGM's set for Jailhouse Rock in 1957. Stoller and Leiber wrote music and lyrics for many of Elvis's movies through the years.

★ SAVORY BEAN BAKE ★

½   **cup molasses**
3   **tablespoons vinegar**
3   **tablespoons prepared mustard**
1   **teaspoon hot pepper sauce**
1   **medium onion, chopped**
3   **16-ounce cans Boston-style baked beans**
1   **16-ounce can kidney beans**

Preheat the oven to 375°. In a large bowl combine all of the ingredients. Pour into a 2½-quart casserole. Bake for 1 hour. Stir and serve! **Serves 4 to 6.**

Jackie Hacker Coleman
Cousin of Elvis Presley

★ THE GREATEST BEAN CASSEROLE ★ IN THE WORLD

4   **slices bacon, chopped**
1   **medium onion, chopped**
1   **16-ounce can baked beans**
1   **16-ounce can red kidney beans, drained**
1   **16-ounce can pinto beans**
¼   **pound Cheddar cheese, cubed**
½   **cup firmly packed brown sugar**
⅓   **cup ketchup**
2   **teaspoons Worcestershire sauce**
    Parmesan cheese, grated

This recipe comes from Donna Dixon.

Preheat the oven to 350°. In a skillet lightly brown the bacon and onions. Add the remaining ingredients except the Parmesan cheese, and pour into a buttered casserole dish. Bake for 30 minutes.

Top with Parmesan cheese and bake 5 minutes more. **Serves about 6.**

Francine and Cecil Blackwood
The Blackwood Brothers

★ BABY, OH BABY BARBECUED BAKED BEANS ★

1   large yellow onion, chopped
7   to 8 pieces bacon, cut into bite-
       sized pieces
2   16-ounce cans baked beans
¾   cup ketchup
¾   cup brown sugar, packed
¼   teaspoon liquid smoke
1   teaspoon fresh crushed garlic, or 3
       cloves, finely crushed

In a large pot mix all the ingredients and cook for 1 hour (or longer, if using a crock pot). Make sure the bacon is fully cooked. Adjust the mixture to taste after 30 minutes by adding another ¼ to ½ cup of barbecue sauce.

Serves 6.

Sandi Daniels
San Diego, California

Elvis and Debra Paget work on their lines on the set of 1956's Love Me Tender.

★ CALICO BEANS ★

1	pound ground chuck
1	12-ounce package bacon, cut into 2-inch pieces
2	16-ounce cans pork and beans
2	16-ounce cans kidney beans
2	16-ounce cans Northern beans
¾	cup ketchup
¾	cup brown sugar
1	teaspoon mustard
1	teaspoon vinegar

In a skillet brown the ground chuck and drain. Semi-fry the bacon and reserve some of the drippings. In a crock pot combine all of the ingredients. Cook on low overnight.

Serves 10 to 12.

Rebecca O'Shields
Jasper, Alabama

IN DECEMBER 1957 ELVIS RECEIVED HIS DRAFT NOTICE FROM THE MEMPHIS DRAFT BOARD. HE REQUESTED A SIXTY-DAY DEFERMENT, SO HE COULD FINISH UP THE FILM *KING CREOLE*. HE REPORTED FOR DUTY MARCH 24, 1958, AS A PRIVATE WITH THE SERIAL NUMBER 53310761. HE GOT HIS FIRST G.I. HAIRCUT ON MARCH 26 AT FORT CHAFFEE, ARKANSAS, AND COMPLETED HIS BASIC TRAINING AT FORT HOOD, TEXAS. AFTER HIS MOTHER'S DEATH, ELVIS WAS ASSIGNED TO DUTY IN GERMANY. HE BROUGHT OVER HIS FATHER AND GRANDMOTHER AND SOME FRIENDS AND PUT THEM UP IN A HOUSE IN THE TOWN OF BAD NAUHEIM. ELVIS SERVED UNTIL MARCH 1960, WHEN HE WAS DISCHARGED AS A BUCK SERGEANT.

★ BUDDY'S BAKED BEANS ★

1 16-ounce can pork and beans
1 12-ounce bottle barbecue sauce
  Ground pepper to taste
2 small onions, chopped
  Dash Cajun seasoning

In a saucepan mix all of the ingredients together and heat on the stove for 10 minutes. This is great for Southern-style barbecue.
Serves 4.

Buddy Early
Donna Presley Early's husband

★ SAUCY BAKED BEANS ★

3 16-ounce cans pork and beans
1 medium onion, chopped
1 medium green pepper, chopped
¼ cup firmly packed dark brown sugar
¼ cup ketchup
2 tablespoons steak seasoning sauce
3 slices bacon

Preheat the oven to 325°. In a 2-quart casserole combine the pork and beans, onion, green pepper, brown sugar, ketchup, and steak seasoning sauce. Top with the bacon slices. Bake uncovered for 1 hour and 30 minutes.
Serves 8 to 10.

Donna Presley Early
First cousin of Elvis Presley

from Elvis Flick to Television (Part Two)

Match the actor who worked with Elvis to the TV series they starred or co-starred in.

TELEVISION FATHERS

1. Carl Betz *(Spinout)*
2. Bill Bixby *(Clambake)*
3. Don Porter *(Live a Little, Love a Little)*
4. Dick Sargent *(Live a Little, Love a Little)*
5. William Schallert *(Speedway)*

A. *Bewitched*
B. *The Courtship of Eddie's Father*
C. *The Donna Reed Show*
D. *Gidget*
E. *The Patty Duke Show*

ANSWERS: 1. C, 2. B, 3. D, 4. A, 5. E

★ READY TEDDY STEWED RED BEANS ★

1 **pound dried red kidney beans**
3 **smoked pork or ham hocks**
1 **pound smoked pork sausage, cut into ½-inch slices**
4 **ribs celery, chopped**
2 **large onions, peeled and chopped**
1 **large green pepper, chopped**
2 **teaspoons minced garlic**
3 **bay leaves**
½ **to 1 teaspoon salt**
½ **teaspoon white pepper**
1 **teaspoon thyme**
1 **teaspoon oregano**
1 **to 2 teaspoons hot sauce**
6 **cups water**

Rinse the beans in a colander under cold running water. Discard any debris or broken beans. Either soak in cold water to cover for 4 to 6 hours, or bring to a boil and allow to sit, covered, for 1 hour. Drain.

Bring the beans and ham hocks to a boil with 2 quarts of fresh water. Simmer covered for 1 hour, then remove the ham hocks and drain the beans. When the ham hocks are cool enough to handle, remove the meat and discard the skin, fat, and bones.

While the beans are simmering, in a skillet brown the sausage over medium heat. Remove the sausage with a slotted spoon and add the celery, onion, green pepper, and garlic to the skillet. Sauté until the onion is translucent. Place the beans, sausage, vegetables, ham meat, bay leaves, salt, pepper, thyme, oregano, and hot sauce in a saucepan with the 6 cups of water. Bring to a boil over medium heat, stirring occasionally, and cook for 45 to 60 minutes over low heat, stirring frequently, especially toward the end of the cooking time. The mixture should be thick and the beans should have started to break up. Discard the bay leaves.

Serves 4 to 6.

Matt Lynn
Quinton, Alabama

★ BEALE STREET BAKED BEANS ★

3 strips bacon, cut into 1-inch pieces
1 medium onion, chopped
1 32-ounce can pork and beans
1 cup brown sugar
1½ cups ketchup

Preheat the oven to 350°. In a skillet sauté the bacon and onion. Drain. In a bowl combine the bacon and onion with the remaining ingredients. Mix well. Make sure there are no lumps of sugar. Pour the mixture into a medium-sized baking pan or dish. Bake for 30 minutes.
Serves 4 to 6.

Betty Jo McMichael
Co-owner, Whistle Stop Cafe
Irondale, Alabama

★ BROWN-EYED HANDSOME MAN ★ BLACK-EYED PEAS

1 12-ounce bag black-eyed peas
5 cups water
  Ham hock (from your local butcher)
  Pepper to taste
1 medium onion, chopped

Wash the beans in a colander. Soak them overnight in a bowl, just covered with water. Drain the water in the morning. Place the beans in a large pot with 5 cups of water. Drop in a ham hock. Sprinkle some pepper to taste. Bring the water to a boil and cook for 3 hours on low to medium heat. Check periodically to make sure the water does not cook out. With a large spoon mash some beans in the pot to create an almost gravy-like effect. Serve with fresh chopped onions.
Serves 4 to 6.

Ovaline Marchant
Vance, Alabama

★ RIDING THE RAINBOW RED RICE ★

4	strips bacon, diced
¼	pound link sausage, diced
1	medium onion, chopped
½	bell pepper, diced
1	rib celery, diced
1	15-ounce can tomato sauce, plus 2½ cans water
	Salt and pepper
1	tablespoon sugar
2½	cups converted rice
¼	cup (½ stick) butter

In a large pot fry the bacon and sausage. Pour off the fat. Remove the meat and sauté the vegetables in the pot. Return the meat to the pot. Add the tomato sauce and the 2½ cans of water. Season with salt and pepper. Bring to a boil. Add the sugar and rice and cook for 45 minutes, covered. Add the butter. Serve with barbecued pork, fish, chicken, pork chops, or sausage.

Serves 6.

Marsha Kinsaul
Dora, Alabama

THE KING AND THE SHERIFF—Elvis enjoys an ice-cold Coca-Cola as he and Faron "The Sheriff" Young pose for this 1958 photo. At left is country music legend Ferlin Husky.

★ MONA LISA MACARONI AND CHEESE ★

1 to 1½ cups uncooked elbow maca-
    roni, rigatoni, or spinach egg
    noodles
¼ cup (½ stick) margarine or butter
1 small onion, chopped
½ teaspoon salt
¼ teaspoon pepper
¼ cup all-purpose flour
1¾ cups milk
8 ounces processed sharp American
    or Swiss cheese, cut into ½-inch
    cubes

Preheat the oven to 375°. Cook the macaroni as directed on the package. In a separate pot melt the margarine or butter and stir in the onion and salt and pepper. Cook over medium heat until the onion is slightly tender. Stir in the flour and cook over low heat, stirring constantly, until the mixture is smooth and bubbly. Remove from the heat and stir in the milk. Heat to boiling, stirring constantly. Boil and stir for 1 minute. Remove from the heat. Stir in the cheese until melted. Place the macaroni in an ungreased 1½-quart casserole. Stir the cheese sauce into the macaroni. Bake uncovered for 30 minutes.
    Serves 4 to 5.

Marlene Nunez
Elvis Country Fan Club

★ MAGICAL MACARONI AND CHEESE ★
CASSEROLE

1 8-ounce package macaroni
3 tablespoons butter or margarine
2 cups milk
1 teaspoon salt
1 teaspoon pepper
2 cups grated Cheddar cheese
3 eggs, slightly beaten

Cook the macaroni in boiling salted water until tender. Drain and rinse with cold water, leaving in the colander to drain. In a saucepan combine the margarine, milk, and seasonings. Cook over medium-high heat until the margarine melts. Let cool.
    Preheat the oven to 350°. In a baking dish layer half of the macaroni and sprinkle with ⅔ of the grated cheese. Top with the remaining macaroni. Add the eggs to the cooled mixture and beat with a wire whisk or cooking spoon. Pour over the layered macaroni and cheese. Sprinkle the remaining cheese over the top. Bake for 30 minutes or until set.
    For extra crispiness, add ⅔ cup of breadcrumbs to the remaining cheese and sprinkle the mixture over the casserole.
    Serves 4.

Betty Jo McMichael
Co-owner, Whistle Stop Cafe
Irondale, Alabama

Elvis Presley taking a break reading fan mail at the Warwick Hotel, NYC between rehearsal and show time of the Tommy and Jimmy Dorsey's Stage Show on CBS-TV, March 17, 1956.

★ WEAR MY RING CRANBERRY DRESSING ★

2	small potatoes
2	cups water
1	rib celery, finely diced
1	small onion, finely diced
½	green pepper, finely diced
3	tablespoons margarine
15	slices bread
1	tablespoon rubbed sage
1	tablespoon poultry seasoning
5	tablespoons chicken soup base
6	ounces fresh cooked cranberries

For a 10-pound turkey or favorite chicken dish.

Preheat the oven to 350°. Peel and cut the potatoes. Place them in the water in a pot on the stove, and boil until tender. Mash them in the remaining water. In a small frying pan sauté the celery, onion, and green pepper in the margarine until tender.

Break the bread into small pieces in a large bowl. Add the sage, poultry seasoning, and soup base and mix it all together. Add the cranberries, vegetables, and potatoes and mix all together. Place in the turkey or place it in a long piece of foil, spreading out the mixture about 3 inches thick. Roll up and close the sides. Bake for 30 minutes.
Serves 8.

Larry Wesley
Collingwood Ontario
Canadian National Elvis Tribute Fan Club

★ STUCK ON YOU ORANGE STUFFING ★

2	cups finely chopped celery
¼	cup butter, melted
3	cups toasted breadcrumbs (about 5 slices, cut into ½-inch cubes)
1	teaspoon grated orange peel
⅔	cup diced orange sections (about 2 medium oranges)
½	teaspoon salt
½	teaspoon poultry seasoning
1	egg, beaten
	Pepper to taste

In a large skillet melt the butter and sauté the celery until tender but not brown. Add the remaining ingredients and then toss lightly.
Serves 4.

Shirley Beattie
Presley-Ites Fan Club
Orlando, Florida

Elvis in 1957, the year he bought Graceland.

Desserts

★ DOWN IN THE ALLEY ★ CHOCOLATE CHIP COOKIES

1   cup (2 sticks) margarine, soft but not melted
½   cup sugar
½   cup firmly packed dark brown sugar
1   egg, beaten
1   teaspoon vanilla extract
3   cups sifted all-purpose flour
     Pinch baking soda
     Pinch salt
1   12-ounce package chocolate chips
1   cup chopped pecans

Preheat the oven to 350°. In a large bowl blend the margarine, sugar, brown sugar, beaten egg, and vanilla together. Slowly mix with an electric mixer on low speed. In a separate bowl mix the flour, soda, and salt. Slowly add the dry ingredients to the liquid mixture. Add the chocolate chips and pecans, and stir all together with a wooden spoon. Drop the batter by the teaspoonful onto a lightly greased cookie sheet. Bake until the cookies are lightly browned.

Makes 2 dozen.

Minnie Lou Mills
Union Springs, Alabama

★ MY FAVORITE CHOCOLATE CHIP COOKIES ★

⅓   cup soft shortening
⅓   cup butter
½   cup sugar
1   cup firmly packed brown sugar, packed
1   egg
1   teaspoon vanilla extract
1½   cups all-purpose flour
½   teaspoon soda
½   teaspoon salt
1   12-ounce package semisweet chocolate pieces
1   cup chopped nuts (optional)

Preheat the oven to 375°. In a large bowl thoroughly mix together the shortening, sugars, egg, and vanilla. Blend in the flour, soda, and salt. Add the chocolate pieces and nuts. Drop the batter by the teaspoonful about 2 inches apart on an ungreased baking sheet. Bake for 8 to 10 minutes or until lightly browned.

Variation: To make chocolate bars, spread the dough evenly in a 9 x 13-inch pan and bake for 20 to 25 minutes. Cut into bars.

Makes about 4 dozen.

Francine and Cecil Blackwood
The Blackwood Brothers

GIDDY-UP—Somebody must have steered Elvis wrong in this scene from the 1968 film Stay Away, Joe.

★ OUT OF SIGHT BUTTERMILK ★ OATMEAL COOKIES

1	cup shortening
1	cup sugar
2	eggs
1	teaspoon vanilla extract
¼	teaspoon salt
1	cup raisins
1	teaspoon baking soda
4	tablespoons buttermilk
2	cups sifted all-purpose flour
2½	cups quick-cooking oats (uncooked)

Preheat the oven to 375°. In a large bowl cream the shortening, sugar, and eggs together. Add the vanilla, salt, and raisins. Stir together well. Dissolve the baking soda in the milk. Alternately add the flour and buttermilk mixture, then add the oats and blend all together well. Drop the batter by the teaspoonful onto a greased cookie sheet. Bake for 12 to 15 minutes.

Makes 3 dozen.

Shirley Beattie
Orlando, Florida
Presley-Ites Fan Club

★ DEVIL IN DISGUISE OATMEAL COOKIES ★

1	cup butter
¾	cup sugar
¾	cup firmly packed dark brown sugar
2	eggs
1¼	cups sifted all-purpose flour
¾	teaspoon ground cinnamon
¾	teaspoon baking soda
½	teaspoon salt
1	teaspoon vanilla extract
3	cups quick-cooking or regular oats (not instant)
1	12-ounce package chocolate-covered raisins
1	cup chopped pecans or walnuts

Preheat the oven to 350°. In a large bowl mix all of the ingredients together. Place small balls of batter onto a nonstick cookie pan. Bake until lightly browned.

Makes 2 dozen.

Nash Presley Pritchett
Aunt of Elvis Presley

★ HIGH-HEEL SNEAKERS SNICKERDOODLES ★

½ cup shortening

¾ cup sugar

1 egg, slightly beaten

1¼ cups sifted all-purpose flour

¼ teaspoon salt

½ teaspoon baking soda

½ teaspoon cream of tartar

2 tablespoons sugar

2 teaspoons ground cinnamon

Preheat the oven to 375°. In a large bowl cream together the shortening, sugar, and egg. Sift the dry ingredients and add to the creamed mixture. Chill the dough for 1 hour.

Roll into balls the size of walnuts. Mix together the 2 tablespoons of sugar and the cinnamon. Place on a plate. Roll the dough balls into the mixture. Place the balls 2 inches apart on the cookie sheet. Bake about 8 to 10 minutes or until they are lightly browned but still soft.
Makes 30.

Linda Kent
Elvis Country Fan Club

★ PATCH IT UP NO-BAKE ★ PEANUT BUTTER COOKIES

2½ cups quick-cooking rolled oats
(uncooked)

½ cup peanut butter

1 teaspoon vanilla extract

½ cup flaked coconut (optional)

½ cup chopped nuts

½ cup milk

2 cups sugar

¼ teaspoon salt

4 tablespoons cocoa

In a large bowl combine the rolled oats, peanut butter, vanilla, coconut, and nuts. In a saucepan combine the milk, sugar, salt, and cocoa. Bring to a boil for just 1 minute, then pour over the rolled oat mixture. Mix until all is blended and then drop by the teaspoonful onto waxed paper. Let stand for 10 minutes or until firm.
Makes 30 cookies.

Shirley Beattie
Presley-Ites Fan Club
Orlando, Florida

★ SNOWBIRD COOKIES ★

1	**15-ounce box any flavor cake mix**
2	**eggs, slightly beaten**
3	**ounces nondairy whipped topping**
1	**cup confectioners' sugar**

Preheat the oven to 350°. In a large bowl mix together the cake mix, eggs, and whipped topping by hand. Chill the dough.

Measure out the batter by the teaspoonful and then roll in the confectioners' sugar. Bake on an ungreased cookie sheet for 10 to 12 minutes. Cool on racks when done.

Makes 2 dozen.

Christy Rogers
Dora, Alabama

Elvis's aunt Nash was in the first grade when this school photo was taken in 1932.

★ HEY HEY HEY HOMEMADE BROWNIES ★

6	tablespoons oil
1	cup sugar
2	eggs, slightly beaten
2	1-ounce squares chocolate, melted
½	to ¾ cup sifted all-purpose flour
½	teaspoon salt
1	teaspoon vanilla extract
¾	cup chopped nuts

Preheat the oven to 325°. In a large bowl stir together the oil, sugar, and eggs. Add the melted chocolate, flour, salt, and vanilla. Stir in the nuts and spread into a shallow, greased 8-inch pan. Bake for 20 to 25 minutes.

Makes 2 dozen.

Varnice Hacker Humphries
Cousin of Elvis Presley

★ FORGET ME NEVER FUDGE BROWNIES ★

⅔	cup margarine, melted
¾	cup cocoa
½	cup water, boiling
2	cups sugar
2	eggs, beaten
1⅓	cups sifted self-rising flour
1½	teaspoons vanilla extract
	Pinch salt
1	cup semi-sweet chocolate chips
1	cup chopped nuts (if desired)

Fudge Icing:

2	cups sugar
1	12-ounce can sweetened condensed milk
½	cup (1 stick) margarine
1	12-ounce bag chocolate chips
1	teaspoon vanilla extract

Preheat the oven to 350°. Grease a 9 x 13-inch pan. In a large bowl blend ⅓ cup of the melted margarine into the cocoa. Add the boiling water. Stir until the mixture thickens. Stir in the sugar, eggs, and remaining ⅓ cup of melted margarine. Stir until all is smooth. Add the flour, vanilla, and salt. Blend all completely. Stir in the chocolate chips and nuts. Pour into the prepared pan. Bake for 20 minutes or until done.

In a saucepan boil the sugar, margarine, and sweetened condensed milk for exactly 2 minutes. Remove the pan from the heat and add the chocolate chips and vanilla. Stir all well and spread over the brownies.

Makes 2 dozen.

Marie Isbell
Sylacauga, Alabama

DON'T FENCE ME IN—*Elvis in a reflective moment in the Western* Stay Away, Joe.

★ JORDANAIRES BEST CHOCOLATE SYRUP ★ BROWNIES

½   **cup (1 stick) butter**
1   **cup sugar**
3   **eggs**
    Dash salt
1   **cup sifted all-purpose flour**
¾   **cup chocolate-flavored syrup**
2   **teaspoons vanilla extract**
¾   **cup chopped walnuts or pecans**

This is the Jordanaires' favorite recipe!

Preheat the oven to 350°. In a large bowl cream together the butter, sugar, and eggs. Add the salt. Stir in the flour, mixing to blend well. Add the chocolate syrup, vanilla, and chopped nuts. Turn the mixture into a well-greased and lightly floured 9-inch square pan. Smooth the top. Bake for about 35 minutes or until a toothpick inserted near the center comes out clean.

Cool in the pan or on a wire rack but loosen at the edges first. Cut into squares. Garnish with pecans or walnut halves or dust with confectioners' sugar.

Makes 16 to 18 brownies.

The Jordanaires

from Elvis flick to Television (Part Three)

Match the actor who worked with Elvis to the TV series they starred or co-starred in.

DRAMA-RAMA

1. Charles Bronson (*Kid Galahad*)
2. Steve Forrest (*Flaming Star*)
3. Victor French (*Charro!*)
4. Angela Lansbury (*Blue Hawaii*)
5. Harry Morgan (*Frankie & Johnny*)
6. Vic Morrow (*King Creole*)
7. Simon Oakland (*Follow That Dream*)

A. *Combat*
B. *Dragnet*
C. *Highway to Heaven*
D. *Kolchak: The Night Stalker*
E. *Man With a Camera*
F. *Murder, She Wrote*
G. *S.W.A.T.*

ANSWERS: 1. E, 2. G, 3. C, 4. F, 5. B, 6. A, 7. D

★ EASY ROCKY ROAD SQUARES ★

2   **8-ounce milk chocolate candy bars**
3   **cups miniature marshmallows**
¾   **cup chopped pecans**

In the bottom of a double boiler heat the water to boiling. Place the candy bars in the top of a double boiler and heat until melted. Stir in the marshmallows and pecans. Spread in a buttered 8-inch square dish. Chill until firm and cut into squares.
    Makes 2 dozen.

Pat Early
Donna Presley Early's mother-in-law

Elvis and the Jordanaires give the troops a beat they can really march to in G.I. Blues.

★ WE'LL BE TOGETHER TOFFEE BARS ★

1	cup (2 sticks) butter
1	cup firmly packed brown sugar
1	egg yolk
2	cups sifted all-purpose flour
6	milk chocolate bars
½	cup chopped pecans

Preheat the oven to 350°. In a large bowl cream the butter and sugar. Add the egg yolk and flour, and mix well. Pat into a 9 x 13-inch pan. Bake for 15 to 20 minutes.

Lay the chocolate bars on top while hot, and sprinkle with nuts. Cool.

Makes 18 bars.

Jackie Hacker Coleman
Cousin of Elvis Presley

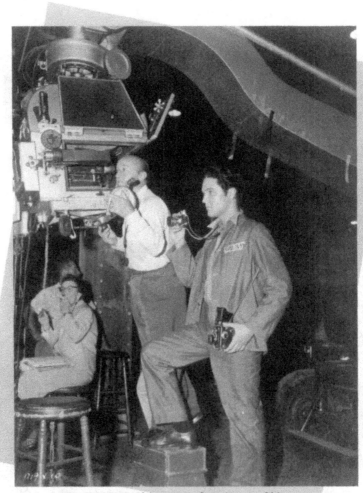

SHUTTERBUG—Elvis snaps a few pictures of his own on the set of MGM's Jailhouse Rock.

★ Let It Be Me Lemon Bars ★

Crust:
- 2 cups sifted all-purpose flour
- 1 cup (2 sticks) margarine
- ½ cup confectioners' sugar

Filling:
- 4 eggs, slightly beaten
  Juice of 4 lemons
- 2 cups sugar
- ¼ cup sifted all-purpose flour
- 1 teaspoon baking powder
- ¼ teaspoon salt

Preheat the oven to 350°. In a medium bowl mix together the flour, margarine, and confectioners' sugar. Roll the dough out on waxed paper as though making a regular pie crust. Place in a 9 x 13-inch pan and lightly press with a fork or your fingers. Bake for 20 minutes.

In a large bowl beat the eggs and add the lemon juice. Add the sugar, flour, baking powder, and salt, and mix all together well. Pour evenly into the baked crust. Return to the oven and bake for an additional 20 to 30 minutes. Let set until cool before cutting into 2-inch squares. Dust a cutting board or waxed paper with confectioners' sugar, and roll the squares to evenly coat with confectioners' sugar.
Makes 2 dozen.

Marva Kaye Ward
Elvis Country Fan Club

★ Temptation Squares ★

Crust:
- 1 large egg, unbeaten
- 1 box Duncan Hines Spice Cake mix
- ½ cup (1 stick) margarine, melted
- ¾ cup chopped pecans

Topping:
- 2 12-ounce cans apricot filling
- 2 cups finely flaked coconut
- 1 12-ounce package butterscotch morsels
- 1 cup medium-coarsely chopped pecans
- 2 14-ounce cans sweetened condensed milk

Place the egg in the bottom of a mixing bowl. Pour the dry cake mix on top of the eggs. Pour the melted margarine over the cake mix. At low speed, mix until it forms a smooth, stiff mixture. Add the chopped pecans and spread lightly on a lightly greased 12 x 18-inch baking sheet.

Over the crust layer in order the apricot pie filling, coconut, butterscotch morsels, pecans, and condensed milk. (Give the sweetened condensed milk a chance to soak in.) Bake at 325° until it begins to bubble and is golden brown.
Makes about 2 dozen.

Sidney Ryan Hicks
Jasper, Alabama

RETURN TO SENDER?—Elvis reads the mail in this scene from Jailhouse Rock,
a film in which he introduced seven new songs in 1957.

★ FAIRY-TALE FUDGE ★

2   **cups sugar**
3   **rounded tablespoons cocoa**
⅛   **teaspoon salt**
½   **cup milk**
¼   **cup white corn syrup**
1   **teaspoon vanilla extract**
½   **cup (1 stick) butter**
1   **cup chopped pecans**

In a saucepan combine all of the ingredients except the pecans. Bring to a boil over medium heat. When the mixture begins to boil, let it cook at full boil for 5 minutes. Remove the mixture from the heat. Beat with an electric beater on full speed for about 2 minutes or until the candy loses its gloss. Add the pecans and stir with a wooden spoon until it is thick. Pour out on a piece of aluminum foil. This will make an 8-inch round at about 1 inch thick.

    Serves 8.

Marian Cocke
Personal nurse for Elvis Presley

★ MY BOY MICROWAVE FUDGE ★

1   **16-ounce box confectioners' sugar**
½   **cup cocoa**
¼   **cup milk**
½   **cup (1 stick) butter or margarine**
1   **tablespoon vanilla extract**
½   **cup chopped pecans**

In a microwave-safe mixing bowl blend together the confectioners' sugar and cocoa. Add the milk and butter, but do not mix them together. Place in the microwave and cook on medium heat for 2 minutes. Remove the bowl from the microwave and stir just to mix the ingredients together. Add the vanilla and the pecans, and stir until blended. Pour into a greased container and place in the freezer for 20 minutes or the refrigerator for 1 hour.

    Makes 2 dozen.

Debbie Busby
Elvis Country Fan Club

★ WAY DOWN WHITE PEANUT BUTTER FUDGE ★

2½	cups sugar
½	cup (1 stick) margarine
¾	cup cream
1	7-ounce jar marshmallow cream
¾	cup peanut butter

In a saucepan mix the sugar, margarine, and cream together and bring to a boil. Boil for 6 minutes, stirring constantly. Add the marshmallow cream and peanut butter. Beat all together until the mixture begins to thicken. Pour into an 8 x 12-inch baking dish and allow to set.

Serves 8 to 10.

Betty Luster
Rogersville, Tennessee

★ AGE OF MIRACLES MICROWAVE ★
PEANUT BRITTLE

1	cup sugar
½	cup white corn syrup
1	cup roasted, salted peanuts
1	teaspoon butter
1	teaspoon vanilla extract
1	teaspoon baking soda

In a 1½-quart casserole, stir the sugar and syrup together. Heat in the microwave oven on high for 4 minutes. Sir in the peanuts. Microwave on high for 3 to 5 minutes, until brown. Add the butter and vanilla to the syrup, blending well. Microwave on high for 1 to 2 minutes more. The peanuts will be lightly browned and the syrup will be very hot. Add the baking soda and gently stir until light and foamy.

Pour the mixture onto a lightly greased or nonstick cookie sheet. Let cool for 30 minutes to 1 hour. When cool, break into small pieces and store in an airtight container.

Note: If raw peanuts are used, add ⅛ teaspoon of salt before microwaving the sugar-syrup mixture.

Makes about 1 pound.

Carlene Sowards
Memphis, Tennessee

★ TENNESSEE TEA CAKES ★

2½ cups sifted all-purpose flour
½ teaspoon baking soda
¾ teaspoon salt
½ cup butter or margarine
½ cup shortening
1 cup sugar
1 teaspoon vanilla extract
1 egg, slightly beaten
2 teaspoons milk

Well, okay, they're from Alabama, but we're neighbors!

Preheat the oven to 400°. In a medium bowl sift together the flour, soda, and salt. In a large bowl cream together the butter or margarine, shortening, sugar, and vanilla. Add the egg and beat until the mixture is fluffy. Stir in the dry ingredients until the mixture is smooth. Blend in the milk. Drop by the teaspoonful onto an ungreased cookie sheet and flatten with a glass or roll out and cut with a biscuit cutter. Sprinkle with sugar or leave plain. Bake for 12 minutes.
    Makes 5 dozen.

Jean Arrington
Union Springs, Alabama

Elvis and friend Eddie Fadal.

★ OLD-FASHIONED SOUTHERN TEA CAKES ★

2¼ cups sifted all-purpose flour
1 cup sugar
1½ teaspoons vanilla extract
2 teaspoons baking powder
¼ cup milk
1 egg, slightly beaten
¾ cup melted butter or margarine

I used to have these with Grandma Alice. We would eat them with a cup of hot tea with lemon and honey and pretend we were dining with the Queen. A little bit of London in rural Alabama!

Preheat the oven to 350°. In a large bowl mix all of the ingredients together until they are moist. Roll out the dough on a floured surface, and cut out to the desired size. Place the cakes on a greased baking sheet. Bake until done, depending on thickness.
Makes 2 dozen.

Edie Hand
Cousin of Elvis Presley

No, this photograph is not from Elvis's Army days or from the 1960 film G.I. Blues. He's merely trying on Army fatigues that a friend gave him for fun before distributing Christmas presents in Nashville.

★ EDGE OF REALITY EIGHTEEN-LAYER ★ CHOCOLATE STACK CAKE

1	cup (2 sticks) butter
1½	cups sugar
6	eggs
3	cups sifted self-rising flour
1	cup milk
1	teaspoon vanilla extract

Icing:

4	1-ounce squares baking chocolate
3	cups sugar
½	cup (1 stick) butter
1	12-ounce can sweetened condensed milk

Preheat the oven to 350°. In a large bowl cream the butter and the sugar together. Add the eggs 1 at a time. Add the flour alternately with the milk. Pour 6 level tablespoons of batter into a 9-inch pan. Bake for 5 minutes. Repeat to make 18 layers.

In a saucepan combine the chocolate, sugar, butter, and sweetened condensed milk and melt over low heat. Spread the icing on the cake layers as soon as you take them out of the oven.

Serves 8.

Ida Mittie Mills
Union Springs, Alabama

★ SMASH HIT CAKE ★

1	egg, slightly beaten
1	15-ounce box yellow cake mix
1	cup chopped pecans
½	cup (1 stick) softened margarine

Topping:

1	8-ounce package cream cheese
1	16-ounce box confectioners' sugar
2	eggs, slightly beaten
1	teaspoon vanilla extract

Preheat the oven to 350°. In a large bowl combine the egg, cake mix, pecans, and margarine, and mix well. Press into the bottom of a 9 x 13-inch cake pan.

In a large bowl combine the cream cheese, confectioners' sugar, eggs, and vanilla. Pour the topping over the cake mixture in the pan. Bake for 30 minutes or until brown.

Serves 8.

Eula Mae Rogers
Cottondale, Alabama

★ NAOMI'S MAYONNAISE CHOCOLATE CAKE ★

1	**cup sugar**
2	**cups all-purpose flour**
½	**cup cocoa**
1½	**teaspoons baking soda**
1	**teaspoon baking powder**
1	**cup real mayonnaise**
1	**cup cold water**
1	**teaspoon vanilla extract**

Preheat the oven to 350°. In a large mixing bowl combine all of the dry ingredients. Add the remaining ingredients and mix until well blended. Pour the batter into a greased and floured 9 x 13-inch cake pan or 2 round layer cake pans. Bake for 25 to 30 minutes until the cake pulls away from the sides of the pan.

To ensure that the cake will come out of the pan, you could line the pan with parchment paper.

Serves 8 to 10.

Francine and Cecil Blackwood
The Blackwood Brothers

The Blackwood Brothers and Elvis: The Southern Gospel Connection

Cecil Stamps Blackwood, only the second baritone in the sixty-three-year history of Southern gospel's famed Blackwood Brothers Quartet, became one of Elvis Presley's best friends when the two were sixteen-year-old high schoolers in Memphis.

The lifelong friendship started in the teen Sunday school class at the First Assembly of God church on Memphis's McLemore Avenue in 1951, several years before Elvis became a gyrating rock 'n' roll sensation.

"He came in late," recalls Blackwood on his initial sighting of Elvis Presley, "and everybody was staring at him because he was dressed a little differently. His hair was different. He had long sideburns, and he was wearing secondhand clothes, bright and loud, a red coat, and white shoes. I got to talking to him and we became friends.

"Elvis loved gospel music and he had been going to see the Blackwood Brothers concerts. He was an admirer of my brother, R. W. Blackwood," says Cecil, who has captured the "Best Baritone" honors numerous times from the Singing News

Awards. Now the sole owner of the Blackwood Brothers Quartet, Cecil and his singers have won nine Grammy Awards and seventeen Dove Awards.

He comes by his vocal talents honestly. The Blackwood Brothers originated in 1934 in Choctaw County, Mississippi, when evangelist Roy Blackwood formed the quartet with his two brothers, Doyle and James, and Roy's oldest son, R. W.

While Cecil's father, brother, and two uncles were performing across the United States in the early 1950s, the teen had formed his own church quartet there at the First Assembly of God. They went by the name of the Songfellows.

"The pastor's son was in the group, and so we were singing around trying to get started. We had a radio program," Cecil recalls. "Elvis had a '41 Lincoln and I had a '48 Studebaker. We became the two most popular guys in class because when it was time to go eat we were the only two with cars.

"Elvis wanted to be a member of the Songfellows, but we didn't have an opening. We would ride around in my Studebaker. We would sing in the car and practice and were good friends, and we would go out to eat at night after church.

"I remember one night we went to Leonard's Barbecue and Elvis and I each had thirteen passengers in our cars. We couldn't go around this one sharp curve because the weight had the springs touching the tires. Everybody had to get out of the cars, so we could get rolling."

As for Elvis's favorite eats as a teen, Cecil says, "His favorite thing was cheeseburgers, always cheeseburgers. We all liked to eat at Leonard's Barbecue on Bellevue and K Barbecue on Crump Boulevard. Those were our two favorite eating spots."

Eventually it appeared that Elvis would be in the Songfellows as one of the members went off to college, but the not-so-studious student quickly got kicked out of school and thus came back to Memphis and the quartet. Elvis was content to wait in the wings and drive along for the fun of it.

Then, on June 30, 1954, tragedy struck the Blackwood Brothers Quartet when an airplane crash in Clanton, Alabama, took the life of Cecil's big brother, R. W.

"After my brother's death I took his place with the Blackwood Brothers, so Elvis came in to sing my part with the Songfellows. This went on for several weeks, but Elvis and Jimmy Hamill, the pastor's son, had several disagreements. Jimmy wanted Elvis to shave his sideburns and he wouldn't. And Jimmy said Elvis couldn't sing harmony.

"Well, one day Elvis came over to my place and had a guitar strapped on his back and he was hot and sweaty, and he said to me, 'I want you to tell Hamill something. Tell him I have signed a contract to sing the blues.' I said, 'Okay, I'll tell him.'

"So Elvis didn't sing with the Songfellows very long. Meanwhile, we were having concerts at Ellis Auditorium in Memphis, and as I would walk through the venue I would see him behind the counter selling Cokes. We would stop and visit.

"Time rocked on," says Cecil, "and all of a sudden Elvis started becoming famous and more famous. We stayed in touch. He would still come to the auditorium to hear us. Whenever we had a concert he would come backstage with ten or twelve of his entourage. He would come out and sing with us

or the Statesmen. Finally he said, 'I can't do it this time. Col. Tom [Parker] said I can't sing unless I'm being paid but I can sit back here and listen.' So he would come back and listen and step out and take a bow and the crowd would go crazy.

"Elvis went off in the Army and then his mother died. We were in South Carolina and he sent an airplane to pick us up and bring us to Memphis so that we could sing at her funeral. We sang about ten of her favorite hymns. He cried on our shoulders and we visited a while.

"Later, after he returned from the Army, there were a number of times we went to visit Graceland and sang way into the night. Over the years he would continue to appear at our concerts. We just stayed friends all the way through," says Cecil with a melancholy tinge to his voice.

"Elvis loved the Blackwood Brothers. We were his favorite singers and gospel was his favorite music. He was completely different from what they played up in the magazines. He was very kind and gentle, soft-spoken as a rule. He always said 'Mr. Blackwood' to James, and 'yes sir and no sir.' He called me Cecil because we were the same age. We didn't know any bad side to Elvis, only the good side."

There was a single incident that has been a thorn in Cecil's side for many years, and for once he would like to set the record straight.

"After Elvis became pretty popular, he would come to church on Sunday nights but would sit up in the balcony out of the way. *Photoplay* magazine came out and interviewed Reverend Hamill, because at the time there was some real controversy about so many churches not liking rock 'n' roll music.

"Reverend Hamill said that Jimmy Hamill and I fired Elvis from the Songfellows because he couldn't sing. That was not the way it was. Jimmy had simply said that Elvis couldn't sing harmony. Elvis laughed about it, but it's something I've never been able to shake. He was a great lead singer, but the misquote was given and we've had to live with it the rest of our lives."

Still, Cecil Blackwood considers those early years with his gospel music–loving friend Elvis Presley to be among his most precious memories.

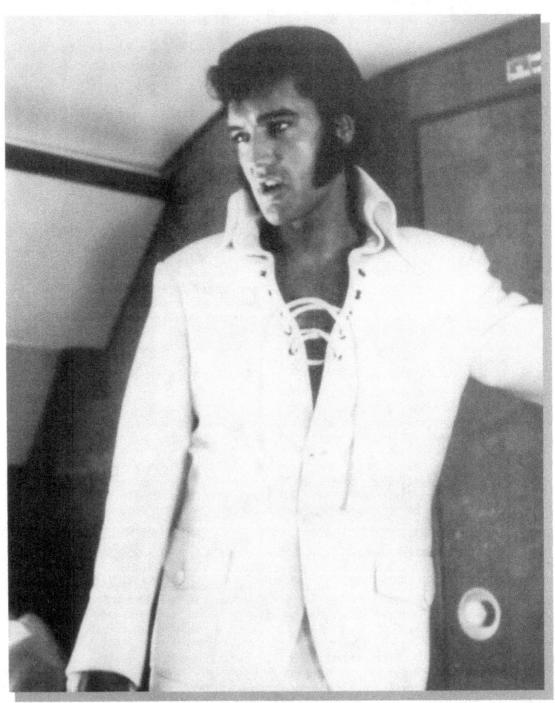

Dressed for a concert.

★ DON'T BE CRUEL DUMP CAKE ★

1 20-ounce can crushed pineapple
1 15-ounce can cherry pie filling
1 cup chopped pecans (optional)
1 15-ounce box yellow cake mix
¾ cup (1½ sticks) margarine

Preheat the oven to 325°. Pour the crushed pineapple, cherry pie filling, and pecans into a 9 x 13-inch pan. Top with the box of yellow cake mix. Do not mix. Simply crumble over the pineapple, cherries, and nuts. Cut the margarine into thin pats and then dot over the entire cake mix. Do not stir! Bake until a cake tester inserted in the center comes out clean. Cool.

Cut into squares and serve with whipped topping or ice cream. **Serves 6 to 8.**

Paula Kennedy
Orlando, Florida
Elvis Presley Continentals of Florida

★ GARBAGE CAKE ★

1 prepared angel food cake
2 3-ounce packages of red gelatin
1 12-ounce can fruit cocktail, drained
2 3-ounce packages of vanilla instant pudding
12 ounces nondairy whipped topping
4 bananas, sliced

Tear up the cake into bite-sized pieces and place in a 9 x 13-inch ungreased pan. Prepare the gelatin according to the package directions. Pour over the cake and refrigerate until set.

Top with the drained fruit. Prepare the pudding according to the directions on the box. Spread the pudding over the fruit and refrigerate for 1 hour.

Top with the sliced bananas and whipped topping. Return to the refrigerator overnight to settle.

Tip: Dip the bananas in citrus juice to prevent them from browning. Any canned fruit can be used. I like sliced peaches in mine. Just make sure to drain well.
Serves 8.

Anna Free
Elvis fan

★ LADY LUCK BUCKET CAKE ★

1 **prepared angel food cake**

1 **12-ounce can strawberry pie filling**

1 **quart fresh strawberries**

1 **3-ounce box vanilla instant pudding mix**

1 **8-ounce container nondairy whipped topping**

Tear the cake into small pieces. Mix the pie filing with the sliced strawberries. Save a few strawberries for garnish. Prepare the pudding according to the directions on the box.

In a bucket or a deep dish place a layer of the cake, a layer of the pudding, a layer of the pie filling mixture, a layer of the whipped topping. Repeat the layers. Garnish with strawberries and refrigerate. **Serves 6 to 8.**

Christy Rogers
Dora, Alabama

Elvis gives his father personal attention from the concert stage.

★ BLUE CHRISTMAS FRUIT CAKE ★

1   **16-ounce box vanilla wafers**
1   **cup pecan halves**
½   **pound candied cherries**
½   **pound candied pineapple**
8   **ounces dates, diced**
½   **cup raisins (optional)**
2   **eggs**
½   **cup sugar**
⅛   **teaspoon salt**
1   **12-ounce can evaporated milk**

Preheat the oven to 325°. Crush the vanilla wafers with a rolling pin. Chop the fruit and nuts, keeping to the side 4 whole cherries, 16 pecan halves, and 12 chunks of pineapple. In a medium bowl mix the chopped fruit and nuts with the vanilla wafer crumbs. In a large bowl beat the eggs well, and then add the sugar, salt, and milk. Add the fruit, nuts, and wafer mix to the egg mixture. Mix all together well with a spoon. Let it stand while you prepare the pan. Insert waxed paper into a loaf pan and let it hang well over the side. Pack the cake mixture in the prepared pan.

Decorate the top of the cake with the reserved cherries, pineapple, and pecan halves. Bake for 1 hour or until done. Watch the fruit and nuts on top as they tend to brown quickly when almost done and can get tough and chewy.
Serves 10.

Paula Kennedy
Orlando, Florida
Elvis Presley Continentals of Florida

Graceland.

★ PLUM GOOD CAKE ★

2   cups sugar

2   cups sifted all-purpose flour

1½   teaspoons baking powder

1   teaspoon salt

1   cup cooking oil

2   4-ounce jars plum baby food, stirred

1   teaspoon ground nutmeg

1   teaspoon ground cinnamon

3   eggs, slightly beaten

1   cup chopped pecans

Icing:

2   teaspoons butter

½   cup firmly packed brown sugar

¼   cup hot water

1   cup confectioners' sugar or as needed

Preheat the oven to 350°. In a large bowl combine the sugar, flour, baking powder, salt, oil, baby food, nutmeg, cinnamon, eggs, and pecans, and beat for 3 minutes. Place in a greased and floured tube pan. Bake for 1 hour or until the top is firm.

In a saucepan melt the butter and add the brown sugar. Mix together well. Add the hot water and boil the mixture together until syrupy. Let cool. Then add enough confectioners' sugar to spread well.
Serves 8.

Paula Kennedy
Elvis Presley Continentals of Florida
Orlando, Florida

Elvis's Platinum Albums

(Sales in excess of a million copies)

Peace in the Valley (1957)
Loving You Volume 2 (1957)
Love Me Tender (1957)
Elvis' Christmas Album (1957), double platinum
Elvis's Golden Records (1958) five times platinum
50,000,000 Elvis Fans Can't Be Wrong (1960)
G.I. Blues (1960)
His Hand in Mine (1961)
Blue Hawaii (1961), double platinum

Elvis' Golden Records Volume 3 (1963)
How Great Thou Art (1967), double platinum
Elvis as Recorded at Madison Square Garden (1972), double platinum
Aloha From Hawaii Via Satellite (1973), double platinum
Moody Blue (1977), double platinum
Elvis in Concert (1977)

★ ANNIE'S POPPY SEED CAKE ★

1   18-ounce box Duncan Hines yellow
    cake mix
1   3-ounce package vanilla instant
    pudding mix
1   2½-ounce jar poppy seeds
2   eggs
¼   cup cooking sherry
¼   cup vegetable oil
1   8-ounce container sour cream

Preheat the oven to 350°. Grease and flour a bundt cake pan. In a medium bowl combine the cake mix, pudding mix, and poppy seeds. In a large bowl mix the eggs, sherry, oil, and sour cream. Add the dry ingredients to the liquid mixture and beat for 3 minutes. Put into the prepared pan. Bake for 40 to 45 minutes.

Let the cake cool for 15 minutes before removing from the pan. Bon appétit!

Anne Sward-Hansen
Salt Lake City, Utah

Anne Sward-Hansen and Edie Hand pause during hospital rounds on
As the World Turns. Anne formerly played the part of series regular
Lila Montgomery, and Edie made a guest appearance.

★ HOUND DOG POUND CAKE ★

3   **cups sugar**
½   **pound butter**
7   **eggs, room temperature**
3   **cups cake flour, sifted twice**
1   **cup whipping cream**
¼   **teaspoon baking soda**
2   **teaspoons vanilla extract**

A favorite of Elvis Presley's.

Cream the sugar and butter. Add the eggs, one at a time, beating after each egg. Add in half of the flour, half of the whipping cream, and then the rest of the flour, the soda, and the rest of the whipping cream. Add the vanilla. Pour in a greased and floured tube pan. Put in a cold oven and turn on at 350°. Bake for 60 to 70 minutes.
Serves 10 to 12.

Ann Morrison
Folkston, Georgia
Elvis Always Fan Club

Elvis the movie heartthrob.

★ THE KING'S POUND CAKE ★

3 cups sugar
1 cup (2 sticks) butter, softened
7 eggs
3 cups well-sifted self-rising flour
1 cup whipping cream
1 teaspoon vanilla extract

Butter and flour a 10-inch tube pan. In a large bowl cream together the sugar and butter. Add the eggs 1 at a time, beating well after each addition. Mix in half of the flour, then the whipping cream, and then the other half of the flour. Add the vanilla. Pour the batter into the prepared pan.

Set in a cold oven and turn the heat to 350°. Bake for 60 to 70 minutes or until a sharp knife inserted into the center of the cake comes out clean. Cool in the pan for 5 minutes, remove, and cool thoroughly.

Serves 8 to 10.

Faye Sanis
Bladensburg, Maryland

Elvis doing what he loved best.

★ Six-Flavor Cake ★

1	teaspoon vanilla extract
1	teaspoon butter flavoring
1	teaspoon rum extract
1	teaspoon lemon flavoring
1	teaspoon coconut flavoring
1	teaspoon almond extract
1	cup milk
1	cup butter
3	cups sugar
½	cup vegetable oil
5	eggs, well beaten
1	teaspoon baking powder
3	cups all-purpose flour

Glaze:

½	cup sugar
½	cup water
1	teaspoon vanilla extract
1	teaspoon butter flavoring
1	teaspoon rum extract
1	teaspoon lemon flavoring
1	teaspoon coconut flavoring
1	teaspoon almond extract

Preheat the oven to 350°. Mix the first 6 ingredients in the 1 cup of milk. In a large bowl cream the butter, sugar, and oil, and then add the eggs. Beat well. In a separate bowl combine the baking powder and flour and then add to the cream mixture, alternating with the milk mixture. Pour the batter into a greased and floured tube pan. Bake for about 1 hour or until done.

In a small saucepan combine the glaze ingredients. Mix thoroughly and heat until the sugar is melted. Pour over the hot cake.

Serves 10 to 12.

Betty Coker
Owner Lisa Marie *and* Hound Dog *airplanes,*
formerly owned by Elvis Presley
Memphis, Tennessee

Movie Quotes

From the movie *Clambake.*

Will Hutchins: "You just said the magic word."
Elvis: "Clambake?"
Will Hutchins: "Yeahhh."

Elvis: "All right, everybody. Get 'em while they're hot—lobsters, clams, chicken, and shrimp."

Elvis: "Mama's little baby loves clambake, clambake."

★ I BELIEVE ICEBOX CRACKER CAKE ★

2   15-ounce packages graham crack-
    ers, crumbled
1   12-ounce can sweetened condensed
    milk
1   cup chopped nuts
1   10-ounce bag miniature marshmal-
    lows
    Chopped cherries, if desired

In a large bowl mix all of the ingredients together. Press into a buttered loaf pan or square pan. Refrigerate overnight.

Keep refrigerated for freshness.

Serves 8 to 10.

Marie Isbell
Sylacauga, Alabama

The King on stage.

★ Stay Away Joe ★ Strawberry Glazed Cheesecake

Crust:

1½ cups graham cracker crumbs, well crushed

¼ cup sugar

⅓ cup melted butter

Cheesecake:

2 8-ounce packages cream cheese, softened

¾ cup sugar

1 teaspoon vanilla extract

3 eggs, slightly beaten

Glaze:

1½ tablespoons cornstarch

1 10-ounce package frozen strawberries, thawed

1 tablespoon lemon juice

In a medium bowl mix together the graham cracker crumbs, sugar, and butter. Press the mixture into a 9-inch pie tin. A pre-made shell can also be used if you want.

Preheat the oven to 350°. In a large bowl blend the cream cheese, sugar, and vanilla. Beat in the eggs until all is smooth and creamy. Pour into the crust and bake for 35 minutes. Set aside and let cool while mixing the glaze.

Place the cornstarch in a saucepan, and place over medium heat. Gradually adding the strawberries, bring to a boil and cook until the mixture thickens and clears. Add the lemon juice and let it cool slightly. Spread the mixture over the cheesecake and refrigerate until ready to serve.

Serves 8 to 10.

Marva Kaye Ward
Elvis Country Fan Club

★ Clambake Cupcake Cheesecakes ★

2 8-ounce packages cream cheese

½ cup sugar

3 eggs, slightly beaten

1 teaspoon vanilla extract

1 11-ounce box vanilla wafers
   Foil muffin cup liners

1 12-ounce can pie fruit filling (your choice of flavor)

Preheat the oven to 325°. Blend the cream cheese and the sugar together. Then beat in the eggs and the vanilla. Line muffin pans with the foil cups. Place a wafer in each cup bottom. Fill each cup ⅔ full with cream cheese mixture. Bake for 10 to 12 minutes. Do not overcook. Top with fruit filling.

Makes 1½ dozen.

Amy Rutledge
Montgomery, Alabama

★ I CAN'T STOP LOVING YOU COCONUT CAKE ★

1   15-ounce box white cake mix
1   12-ounce can sweetened condensed
     milk
1   4-ounce can cream of coconut, well
     shaken
1   8-ounce bag flaked coconut
1   12-ounce container nondairy
     whipped topping
1   8-ounce carton sour cream
½   cup sugar

Prepare the cake batter according to the box directions and bake in a 9 x 13-inch pan.

Poke holes in the cake with a fork while still warm. Allow the cake to cool. In a medium bowl combine the sweetened condensed milk and the cream of coconut. Pour it onto the cake and refrigerate.

In a large bowl mix the whipped topping, sour cream, and sugar together. Spread on top for frosting. Sprinkle the coconut flakes on top.

Serves 8 to 10.

Darolyn Arrington
Montgomery, Alabama

The living room of Graceland as it looked when Elvis died.

★ ALL SHOOK UP CAKE ★

1	15-ounce package yellow cake mix
1	20-ounce can crushed pineapple, drained
1	cup sugar
1	3-ounce box vanilla instant pudding
2	bananas
1	8-ounce container nondairy whipped topping
1	8-ounce bag coconut flakes
1	cup chopped nuts

Prepare the cake according to the directions on the box and bake in a 9 x13-inch pan. Pour the pineapple into a saucepan, add the sugar, and then simmer for 5 to 10 minutes, stirring frequently. When the cake is done, poke holes in it and pour the pineapple mixture over it. Let cool.

Prepare the pudding according to the directions on the box. Pour it evenly over the cake. Place a layer of bananas on top of the pudding, and top that with the whipped topping. Sprinkle coconut and chopped nuts over the whipped topping.

Serves 6 to 8.

Linda Kent
Elvis Country Fan Club

★ JUNGLE ROOM BANANA SPLIT CAKE ★

1½	cups (3 sticks) margarine, 1 melted and 2 softened
2	cups graham cracker crumbs
3	cups sifted confectioners' sugar
½	cup half and half
5	medium or 3 large bananas
1	15-ounce can pineapple tidbits in own syrup
1	8-ounce container nondairy whipped topping
½	cup chocolate syrup
½	cup chopped pecans
½	cup chopped maraschino cherries

In a medium bowl combine the ½ cup of melted margarine and the graham cracker crumbs. Mix together well and pack into a 9 x 13-inch pan or a baking dish. Refrigerate.

In a mixing bowl combine the softened margarine, confectioners' sugar, and half and half. Beat at medium speed for 10 minutes. Spread the filling over the chilled crust. Cut the bananas into ¼-inch slices and place into the filling, pressing slightly. Drain the pineapple tidbits and chop into smaller pieces. Spread the pineapple on top of the bananas. Top with the whipped topping, and freeze.

Remove from the freezer 1 hour before serving and garnish with chocolate syrup, chopped pecans, and maraschino cherries.

Note: Make sure that you drain as much of the water from the pineapple tidbits as possible. After draining, press with a spoon to squeeze out more juice, chop the tidbits, and then drain again.

Serves 6 to 8.

Betty Jo McMichael
Co-owner, Whistle Stop Cafe
Irondale, Alabama

★ PUNCH BOWL CAKE ★

1   15-ounce package yellow or white
    cake mix
6   to 8 bananas, sliced
2   12-ounce cans blueberry pie filing
2   12-ounce cans cherry or strawberry
    pie filling
1   16-ounce container nondairy
    whipped topping
1   20-ounce can crushed pineapple
½   cup coconut flakes
½   cup chopped pecans
½   cup chocolate syrup

Prepare and bake the cake mix according to the directions on the box. Separate the cake into 4 equal parts. Crumble 1 part into the bottom of a punch bowl. Place one-third of the sliced bananas throughout the cake wherever you like. Then top with a layer of pie filling and then a layer of whipped topping.

Repeat 2 more times, then crumble the last part of the cake on top, layer the pie filling, the pineapple, and then the whipped topping. Finally, garnish with the coconut, pecans, and the chocolate syrup.

Serves 8.

Marlene L. Nunez
Elvis Country Fan Club

WHEN ONE WOMAN NEEDED A NEW WHEEL-
CHAIR, ELVIS BOUGHT IT FOR HER AND PERSON-
ALLY DELIVERED IT. AND WHEN ELVIS WAS DOING
ONE OF THE THINGS HE LIKED TO DO BEST—SHOP
FOR NEW CARS—HE WOULD SPOT A YOUNG COU-
PLE OR ELDERLY WOMAN IN THE SHOWROOM
AND ASK THEM WHAT COLOR THEY LIKED. THEY
WOULD RESPOND, THINKING THEY WERE JUST
CHATTING. THEN ELVIS WOULD PURCHASE THEM
THE CAR IN THEIR PREFERRED COLOR.

Elvis in action.

★ PIÑA COLADA CAKE ALOHA ★

1   15-ounce box yellow cake mix
1   8-ounce can cream of coconut
1   12-ounce can sweetened condensed
      milk
1   20-ounce can crushed pineapple,
      drained
1   8-ounce container nondairy
      whipped topping

Prepare and bake the yellow cake mix according to the directions on the box. In a separate bowl mix the cream of coconut and the sweetened condensed milk. Punch holes in the baked cake and pour the mixture over the top. Add the crushed pineapple on the top. Cover the cake with the whipped topping and refrigerate.

Serves 6 to 8.

Marlene L. Nunez
Elvis Country Fan Club

★ BLUE HAWAII PINEAPPLE ★ UPSIDE-DOWN CAKE

2   tablespoons butter or margarine
¼   cup firmly packed brown sugar
1   8½-ounce can sliced pineapple
      (four slices), drained
1½ cups packaged biscuit mix
¼   cup sugar
2   tablespoons shortening
1   teaspoon vanilla extract
1   egg
¾   cup milk

Preheat the oven to 350°. In an 8-inch square pan melt the butter or the margarine over low heat. Sprinkle the brown sugar evenly over the bottom of the pan. Place 1 whole pineapple slice in the center of the pan. Cut the remaining 3 slices in half. Arrange the halves, cut side out, around the edge of the pan.

In a medium bowl combine the biscuit mix, sugar, shortening, vanilla, egg, and ½ cup of the milk. Beat for 1 minute at medium speed on an electric mixer or vigorously beat by hand. Add the remaining ¼ cup of milk. Beat for 1 minute. Pour the batter carefully over the pineapple in the pan. Bake for 35 minutes or until the cake springs back when the center is lightly touched with your fingertip.

Remove from the oven and let stand in the pan for 1 minute. Loosen the cake from around the sides of the pan with a spatula or a thin-bladed knife. Place a large serving plate face down over the cake. Turn upside down. Remove the pan and cut in squares while still warm. Garnish the cake with maraschino cherry halves if desired.

Serves 8.

Sue Hacker Hardesty
Cousin of Elvis Presley

★ SOUND ADVICE SOUR CREAM CAKE ★

1   **cup (2 sticks) butter**
2   **cups sugar**
4   **eggs**
2   **cups sifted all-purpose flour**
1   **teaspoon baking powder**
½   **teaspoon salt**
½   **pint sour cream**
3   **tablespoons firmly packed brown sugar**
2   **teaspoons ground cinnamon**
¼   **cup chopped pecans**
¼   **cup raisins**

Preheat the oven to 350°. In a large bowl cream the butter and the sugar. Add the eggs 1 at a time. Add the flour, baking powder, and salt. Add the sour cream and mix well. Pour half of the batter into a bundt pan. In a small bowl combine the brown sugar, cinnamon, pecans, and raisins. Sprinkle the mixture over the batter. Pour the rest of the batter on top. Bake for 1 hour.

Serves 8 to 10.

Marian Cocke
Personal nurse for Elvis Presley

★ SENSATIONAL SOUR CREAM COFFEE CAKE ★

1   **cup chopped pecans**
2   **tablespoons firmly packed brown sugar**
2   **teaspoons ground cinnamon**
1   **cup (1 stick) butter or margarine**
1   **cup sugar**
2   **eggs, slightly beaten**
2   **cups sifted all-purpose flour**
1   **teaspoon baking powder**
1   **teaspoon baking soda**
1   **8-ounce carton sour cream**
4   **tablespoons confectioners' sugar**
1   **tablespoon water**

Preheat the oven to 375°. Combine the pecans, brown sugar, and cinnamon. Stir together well, and set aside. In a large bowl cream the butter and gradually add in the sugar, beating until the mixture is fluffy. Add the eggs and beat all well.

In a separate bowl combine the flour, baking powder, and soda. Add the dry ingredients to the creamed mixture alternately with the sour cream, beginning and ending with the flour mixture. Spoon half of the batter into a greased and floured 10-inch bundt pan. Sprinkle half of the pecan mixture over the batter. Repeat the layers. Bake for 35 to 45 minutes or until done. Cool for 5 minutes in the pan on a wire rack. Invert the cake onto a serving plate and let cool. Combine the confectioners' sugar with the water to make a glaze, and then drizzle over cake. Store overnight in an airtight container.

Serves 6 to 8.

Donna Roberts
Montreal, Quebec

★ AMERICA THE BEAUTIFUL APPLE CAKE ★

2   cups sugar
1½   cups cooking oil
3   eggs, slightly beaten
2   teaspoons vanilla extract
3   cups all-purpose flour
1   teaspoon baking soda
1   teaspoon salt
1   cup chopped nuts
3   cups chopped fresh apples

Glaze:
1   cup firmly packed brown sugar
¼   cup milk
½   cup (1 stick) butter or margarine
1   8-ounce container nondairy
         whipped topping

Preheat the oven to 350°. In a large bowl mix together the sugar, oil, and eggs. In a separate bowl sift the flour, soda, and salt together. Add the dry ingredients to the liquid mixture. Fold in the nuts and apples. Bake for 1 hour.

In a saucepan combine the sugar, milk, and butter or margarine and heat for 3 minutes. Pour over the cake and let stand for 2 hours before serving. Dot with dollops of whipped topping.

Serves 6 to 8.

Gay Neel Wilhite
Elvis fan

Elvis enjoys a moment in Germany during his hitch with the Army.

★ ADAM AND EVIL APPLE CAKE ★

⅔   cup oil
2   eggs
3   cups apples, peeled and chopped
      (about 3 medium apples)
1½ cups sugar
¾   cup self-rising flour
1   teaspoon ground cinnamon
¼   teaspoon allspice
1   teaspoon vanilla extract
1   cup chopped nuts

Preheat the oven to 325°. Grease a 9 x 13-inch baking pan. Beat the oil and eggs until foamy. Stir in the apples and sugar. In a separate bowl mix the flour, cinnamon, and allspice. Stir in the apple mixture. Stir in the vanilla and nuts. Pour into the prepared pan and bake for 45 minutes or until the top springs back.

Serves 10 to 12.

Verter Sylvain
Elvis Memories Fan Club
Zwijndrecht, Belgium

★ VERY NICE ORANGE SLICE CAKE ★

1   teaspoon baking soda
½   cup buttermilk
1   cup butter
2   cups sugar
4   eggs
1   teaspoon salt
3½ cups sifted all-purpose flour
2   cups chopped nuts
1   pound orange slice candy, finely
      chopped
1   8-ounce box dates, finely chopped
1   7-ounce can flaked coconut

Orange Sauce Topping:
1   cup orange juice
2   cups confectioners' sugar

Preheat the oven to 250°. Dissolve the soda in the buttermilk. In a separate bowl cream the butter and the sugar together. Add the 4 eggs 1 at a time, mixing well after each addition. Add the salt, half of the flour, and the buttermilk mixture.

Roll the nuts, candy, and dates in the remaining half of the flour. Add the rolled nuts, candy, and dates to the butter/sugar mixture. Add the coconut and mix. Pour the mixture into a greased tube pan. Bake for 2 hours and 30 minutes.

While the cake is baking, combine the orange juice and confectioners' sugar. After removing the pan from the oven, place the cake on a serving dish. Spoon the topping over the hot cake.

Serves 8 to 10.

Rhea Marie Edenfield
Elvis, Forever and Always

★ GOOD ROCKIN' GRAHAM CRACKER CAKE ★

3   eggs, slightly beaten
½   cup softened butter
1   cup sugar
1   tablespoon vanilla extract
½   cup sifted all-purpose flour
     Pinch salt
½   teaspoon baking soda
2½ cups graham cracker crumbs
¾   cup milk

Frosting:
½   cup butter, softened
     Milk
     Confectioners' sugar
     Cocoa

Preheat the oven to 375°. In a large bowl mix together the eggs, butter, sugar, and vanilla. Add the flour, salt, and baking soda, and stir well. Then add the graham cracker crumbs and milk slowly until they are all combined. Stir well. Line the bottoms of 2 cake pans with waxed paper. Pour the batter into the pans. Bake for 25 to 35 minutes or until done.

In a large mixing bowl cream the butter. Add the milk and confectioners' sugar to your liking. Add cocoa to taste if desired.

Serves 8 to 10.

Pat Early
Donna Presley Early's mother-in-law

★ BEST FOR LAST STRAWBERRY CAKE ★

2   10-ounce packages frozen strawberries, reserving 1 cup strawberry juice
1   3-ounce package strawberry gelatin
1   package yellow cake mix
4   eggs
½   cup vegetable oil
1   cup shredded coconut
1   cup chopped pecans

Icing:
½   cup (1 stick) butter, softened
1   16-ounce package confectioners' sugar
     Strawberries
1   cup chopped pecans
1   cup shredded coconut

Preheat the oven to 350°. Place the strawberries in a colander to drain, catching the juice in a pan. In a bowl mix the strawberry gelatin with the cake mix. Add 1 cup of the reserved juice, the eggs, and the oil. Mix well. Add the coconut and pecans and pour into greased 9-inch cake pans. Bake for 25 to 30 minutes or until a toothpick inserted in the middle of the cake comes out clean.

In a large bowl mix the butter and confectioners' sugar. Wash and blot the strawberries well with a paper towel to remove the surface juice. Mix the strawberries, pecans, and coconut with the butter-sugar mixture. (If it is not firm enough, add some more sugar.) Place in the refrigerator while the cake is cooling. (The icing is better if left in the refrigerator overnight prior to use.)

Serves 10 to 12.

Betty Coker
Owner of Lisa Marie and Hound Dog airplanes,
formerly owned by Elvis Presley
Memphis, Tennessee

★ LUSCIOUS RED VELVET ELVIS CAKE ★

Cake:

2½ cups sifted all-purpose flour

1½ cups sugar

1   teaspoon baking soda

1   teaspoon cocoa

1   cup buttermilk

1½ cups oil

1   teaspoon vinegar

2   eggs, slightly beaten

½   ounce red food coloring

1   teaspoon vanilla extract

Frosting:

½   cup (1 stick) soft margarine

1   8-ounce package cream cheese

1   16-ounce box confectioners' sugar

½   teaspoon vanilla extract

1   cup chopped nuts

Preheat the oven to 350°. In a large bowl combine all of the cake ingredients and bake for 25 to 30 minutes. Let cool. In a medium bowl combine the frosting ingredients until creamy and smooth. Frost between the layers and on the top and sides of cake.
Serves 8 to 10.

Kim Blackburn Poss
Cousin of Elvis Presley

---

from Elvis Flick to Television (Part Four)

Match the actor who worked with Elvis to the TV series they starred or co-starred in.

SITCOM U.S. MALES

1. Jack Albertson *(Kissin' Cousins)*
2. Ed Asner *(Change of Habit)*
3. Pat Buttrum *(Roustabout)*
4. Jackie Coogan *(Girl Happy)*
5. William Demarest *(Viva Las Vegas)*
6. Gale Gordon *(Speedway)*
7. Pat Harrington *(Easy Come, Easy Go)*
8. Dean Jones *(Jailhouse Rock)*
9. Howard McNear *(Blue Hawaii)*
10. Alejandro Rey *(It Happened at the World's Fair)*

A. *The Addams Family*
B. *The Andy Griffith Show*
C. *Chico and the Man*
D. *Ensign O'Toole*
E. *The Flying Nun*
F. *Green Acres*
G. *The Lucy Show*
H. *The Mary Tyler Moore Show*
I. *My Three Sons*
J. *One Day at a Time*

ANSWERS: 1. C, 2. H, 3. F, 4. A, 5. I, 6. G, 7. J, 8. D, 9. B, 10. E

Elvis cuddles with leading lady Mary Tyler Moore in a scene from Change of Habit, *released in 1969.*

★ GRANDMA'S PIE CRUST ★

4 cups sifted all-purpose flour
1¾ cups shortening
1 egg, slightly beaten
1 tablespoon vinegar
½ cup ice water
1 tablespoon sugar
1 teaspoon salt

Preheat the oven to 450°. In a large bowl mix all of the ingredients together. Roll out the crust. Place in a pie pan and pierce with a fork. Bake for 6 to 8 minutes.
Makes 5 to 6 crusts.

Verna Melohn
Elvis fan

Elvis backstage in one of his classic performing outfits.

★ CLASSIC CHESS PIE ★

4	eggs, slightly beaten
2	cups sugar
1	cup (1 stick) butter or margarine
1	teaspoon cornmeal
	Ground nutmeg to taste
1	unbaked 9-inch pie crust

Preheat the oven to 300°. In a large bowl mix all of the ingredients thoroughly. Pour into the pie crust. Bake for about 1 hour.
Serves 8.

Mary Tom Speer Reid
The Speer Family

IN 1969, ELVIS HIT LAS VEGAS LIKE A ROCKET SHIP—PLAYING TWO SHOWS A NIGHT FOR TWENTY-NINE NIGHTS AND PACKING TWO THOUSAND PEOPLE INTO THE HOUSE EACH SHOW. FOR HIS FABULOUS SUCCESS, ELVIS WAS PRESENTED A GOLD BELT FOR SETTING THE "WORLD'S CHAMPIONSHIP ATTENDANCE RECORD."

★ CHOCOLATE LOVER'S CHESS PIE ★

4	heaping tablespoons cocoa
1½	cups sugar
2	eggs, beaten
½	cup pecan halves
¼	cup (½ stick) butter
½	cup unsweetened evaporated milk
½	cup coconut
1	9-inch pie crust

Preheat the oven to 400°. In a large bowl mix together the cocoa, sugar, eggs, pecans, butter, evaporated milk, and coconut. Pour into the pie crust. Bake for 30 minutes.

Cool and serve with a scoop of vanilla ice cream.
Serves 6 to 8.

Shirley Beattie
Presley-Ites Fan Club
Orlando, Florida

★ BETTY'S BEBOPPIN' RITZ CRACKER PIE ★

3   egg whites
1   cup sugar
1   teaspoon baking powder
    Dash salt
20 Ritz crackers, finely crushed
¾   cup chopped walnuts
1   teaspoon vanilla extract
    Whipped cream

Preheat the oven to 350°. In a large bowl beat the egg whites until stiff. Fold in the sugar, baking powder, and salt. Combine the cracker crumbs and walnuts. Fold very gently into the egg white mixture. Add the vanilla. Pour into a buttered 8-inch pie plate. Bake for 25 to 30 minutes.

Cool and top with whipped cream.

Serves 6 to 8.

Betty and Harvey Bullock

Courtesy of Harvey Bullock

On the set of Girl Happy are (left to right) screenwriters Ray Allen and Harvey Bullock, producer Joe Pasternak, and Elvis.

The Renowned Screenwriter Harvey Bullock Remembers Working with Elvis:

Ray Allen and I were at MGM writing our first film, which was being produced by the legendary Pandro Berman. We had a drab office in the Thalberg building, a writer's mecca during the roaring Thirties. But the halls once filled with boisterous film writers were now empty and echoing. The only other occupant on the entire ground floor was (also legendary) producer Joe Paternak.

We had some lunches with Joe. He was most affable and entertaining—with riveting stories of the old big studio days. We were finishing our script for Berman when suddenly Joe Pasternak came into our run-down room and inquired in a rich Hungarian accent, "I have to do a film with Elvis Presley. You boys want to write it?"

We fell all over ourselves accepting, and thus came *Girl Happy*.

But the real story to us was not the one filmed. It was the one *Variety* could have headlined: "Famed Producer Seeks out Rookie Writers to Offer Plum Assignment." Unheard of.

When we took the job, Ray and I knew very little about Elvis. We assumed he was the stereotypical rock star—laid back, indifferent, undisciplined. We were in for a huge surprise.

The film had long beach scenes that actually were shot at night. The dancers and extras were soon exhausted. But Elvis continued to do every take and re-take at top energy—until after midnight and with no complaints and all while incorporating changes by the director. We will always remember and respect Elvis as a hard-working, talented professional.

Elvis knew whatever character he played should be gentle with women and strongly bonded with men. Therefore he was dubious of a scene in *Girl Happy* requiring him to wear a dress (as a disguise so that he could sneak into a women's jail).

We and director Boris Sagal assured Elvis that the scene would not be "campy" or effeminate. He reluctantly agreed. But he made sure that he would keep his masculinity clear. He okayed a shapeless all-black dress, folded his arms and (I think) spoke in a deeper voice. He got away with it beautifully. Elvis knew his role and what his boundaries were.

Harvey Bullock also remembers Colonel Parker:

Colorful Colonel Parker, Elvis's agent and mentor, was a wizard at making money out of anything. To celebrate finishing the Elvis script, Joe Pasternak took us to lunch at the MGM commissary. Joe was pleased with the script and steered us to a booth where Colonel Parker was lunching. Joe introduced us, saying, "The boys have just finished the script. Would you like to read it?"

The Colonel never missed a beat. Without even looking up, he said firmly, "That's extra."

★ GOLDEN OLDIES OLD-FASHIONED ★ CHOCOLATE PIE

2½ cups sugar
3 tablespoons cocoa
5 tablespoons sifted all-purpose flour
Pinch salt
3 eggs
2 cups milk
2 tablespoons vanilla extract
1 ready-made 9-inch shell

This is a family favorite during the holidays!

In a large bowl mix 2 cups of the sugar, cocoa, flour, and salt together. Separate the egg yolks from the whites. Beat the egg yolks with 2 cups of milk. Combine with the dry ingredients. Add 1 tablespoon of the vanilla extract to the mixture. Pour the mixture into a large iron skillet and cook until it is thickened. Pour into pie crust and let cool.

Beat the egg whites until stiff. Add the remaining ½ cup of sugar and 1 tablespoon of vanilla. Continue beating the egg whites until they are firm. Spread over the pie. Turn the oven on to broil. Place the pie in the oven and let brown for 2 or 3 minutes.

Serves 6 to 8.

Velon Hood Hacker
Cousin of Elvis Presley

Presley family members in this 1996 photo are cousins Donna Presley Early (far left), Danny Hacker (third from left), Jackie Hacker Coleman (fourth from left), Edie Hand (third from right), and Velon Hood Hacker (second from right). Also pictured are members of TCM for Elvis Fan Club, including group president Michelle Elaine (in back between Jackie and Edie), Elizabeth Brock (second from left), and Earl White (far right).

★ FAMILY FAVORITE FRUIT PIE ★

¼   cup lemon juice

1   12-ounce can sweetened condensed milk

1   15-ounce can pie fruit filling (cherries, blueberries, and strawberries)

1   20-ounce can chopped pineapple

¼   cup chopped pecans, optional

1   8-ounce container nondairy whipped topping

2   9-inch graham cracker pie crusts

In a large bowl mix the lemon juice and sweetened condensed milk together. Fold in the fruit and the nuts. Mix well and fold into the nondairy whipped topping. Pour into the pie crusts and let chill for several hours.

Each pie serves 8 to 10.

Pat Early
Donna Presley Early's mother-in-law

Elvis on stage during a road show in Florida in the 1950s.

★ ELVIS ALWAYS SWEET POTATO PIE ★

3	eggs, beaten
1	cup brown sugar, packed
1	cup evaporated milk (or whole milk)
1	teaspoon ground cinnamon
½	teaspoon ground nutmeg
½	teaspoon salt
1	teaspoon vanilla extract
1	teaspoon almond extract
3	tablespoons melted butter or margarine
1½	cups mashed sweet potatoes
1	unbaked pie shell

Preheat the oven to 375°. In a bowl combine the first 6 ingredients and mix well. Add the vanilla and almond extracts and the butter to the egg mixture. Beat with an electric mixer. Add the mashed sweet potatoes and continue to mix. Pour into the pie shell. Bake for 50 to 60 minutes or until a knife inserted in the middle of the pie comes out clean. Cool and serve with whipped topping, if desired.

Serves 8 to 10.

Elvis Always Fan Club

Photo courtesy of Pat Tuggle

Elvis looking relaxed while stationed in Germany during his hitch in the Army.

★ SWEDISH SWIVEL PIE ★

1	egg
½	teaspoon vanilla extract
½	cup all-purpose flour
1	cup apples, chopped
⅜	cup sugar
⅜	cup brown sugar
	Pinch salt
1	teaspoon baking powder
1	cup chopped pecans

Preheat the oven to 350°. In a mixing bowl stir all of the ingredients together and pour into a greased glass pie plate. Bake for 30 minutes. After it cools, serve with whipped topping and nuts or warm with ice cream.

Serves 6 to 8.

Mary Tuggle
Trussville, Alabama

Pictured with Elvis is fellow soldier Bobby Tuggle.

Photo courtesy of Pat Tuggle

★ TUTTI FRUTTI PIE ★

1   3-ounce package peach gelatin
⅔   cup boiling water
2   cups ice cubes, crushed
1   8-ounce container nondairy
      whipped topping
2   cups peaches or nectarines, diced
1   9-inch graham cracker or vanilla
      wafer pie crust

In a large bowl dissolve the gelatin in boiling water, stirring for 1 minute. Add the ice cubes and stir until thick, for about 3 minutes. Remove any unmelted ice cubes. Blend in the whipped topping, and add the fruit. Pour into the pie crust and chill for 3 hours.
   Serves 8.

Emily McGriff
Dora, Alabama

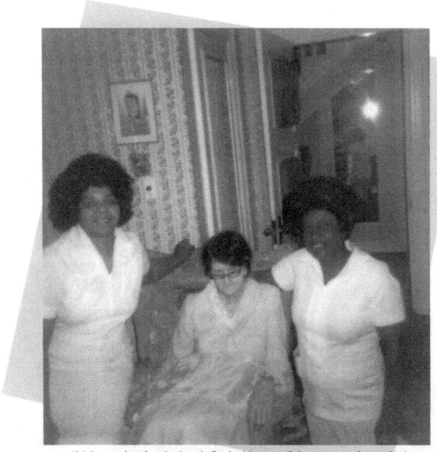

Elvis's grandmother Dodger is flanked by two of the women who cooked for the Presley family at Graceland: Nancy Rook (left) and Mary Jenkins.

★ COUNTRY BUTTERMILK PIE ★

3	**tablespoons sifted all-purpose flour**
1½	**cups sugar**
½	**cup (1 stick) butter (do not use margarine)**
3	**eggs, slightly beaten**
2	**cups buttermilk**
1	**unbaked 9-inch pie crust**

Preheat the oven to 350°. In a large bowl mix the flour and the sugar together. Cream with the butter. Add the beaten eggs. Add the buttermilk last. Pour the mixture into the unbaked pie crust. Bake until a knife inserted into the center of the pie comes out clean.
    Serves 8 to 10.

Debbie Busby
Elvis Country Fan Club

Complete the Words or Letters to These Songs Sung by Elvis

1. _ _ _ _ _ _ _ _ _ _ HILL
2. _ _ _ _ _ _ _ _ _ LAND
3. DO THE _ _ _ _
4. HOT _ _ _
5. _ _ _ BALAYA
6. MONEY _ _ _ _ _ _
7. OLD _ _ _ _ _ _ _ _ _ _ ('s)
8. _ _ _ _ _ _ _ _ _ ANNIE
9. QUEENIE WAHINE'S _ _ _ _ _ _
10. _ _ _ _ _ _ _ BORD
11. SONG OF THE _ _ _ _ _ _
12. THREE _ _ _ _ PATCHES
13. TUTTI _ _ _ _ _ _

ANSWERS:

1. BLUEBERRY
2. COTTON CANDY
3. CLAM
4. DOG
5. JAM
6. HONEY
7. MacDONALD
8. POLK SALAD
9. PAPAYA
10. SMORGAS
11. SHRIMP
12. CORN
13. FRUTTI

★ BUDDY'S LEMON ICEBOX PIE ★

2   12-ounce cans sweetened condensed milk

Juice of 7 lemons

2   egg yolks

1   graham cracker pie crust

1   8-ounce container nondairy whipped topping

In a large bowl combine the sweetened condensed milk, lemon juice, and egg yolks. Blend the ingredients together and pour into the graham cracker pie crust. Place in the refrigerator for at least 4 hours. For better results, leave overnight.

Remove the pie from the icebox, and spread with the nondairy whipped topping to make a delicious dessert.

Serves 6 to 8.

Buddy Early
Donna Presley Early's Husband

ELVIS'S GRANDMA DODGER LOVED HER APRONS. SHE HAD DOZENS, INCLUDING SPECIAL CHRISTMAS AND EASTER APRONS. SHE HAD A DIFFERENT ONE FOR EVERY DAY OF THE WEEK. ELVIS AND OTHER MEMBERS OF THE FAMILY BOUGHT THEM FOR HER. DODGER HAD ANOTHER LIKING AS WELL: SHE LIKED TO HAVE HER BED AIRED OUT. EVERY WEEK, SHE WOULD HAVE IT TOTED OUT OF HER ROOM AND INTO THE YARD AT GRACELAND WHERE IT WOULD AIR OUT BENEATH THE WARM, SOUTHERN SUN. NEEDLESS TO SAY THIS REQUIRED A LOT OF MUSCLE POWER FROM THE BOYS. BUT NOTHING WAS TOO GOOD FOR DODGER.

★ LOVING YOU LAYERED CHOCOLATE PIE ★

First Layer:

1½	cups sifted all-purpose flour
1½	cups margarine, melted
½	cup chopped nuts

Second Layer:

1	8-ounce package cream cheese, softened
1	cup confectioners' sugar
1	cup nondairy whipped topping

Third Layer:

2	3-ounce packages instant chocolate pudding mix
3	cups milk

Fourth Layer:

4	ounces nondairy whipped topping
1	cup chopped pecans

Preheat the oven to 350°. In a medium bowl mix the flour, margarine, and nuts, and spread in a 9 x 13-inch pan. Bake until brown. Let cool.

In a medium bowl mix the cream cheese, confectioners' sugar, and whipped topping, and spread over the first layer.

In a large bowl combine the pudding mix and milk, and mix for 2 minutes at low speed with mixer. Spread on top of the second layer.

Spread the whipped topping on top and sprinkle with the chopped pecans. Refrigerate.

Serves 8.

Jean Arrington
Union Springs, Alabama

★ C. C. RIDER COCONUT CARAMEL PIE ★

¼	cup (½ stick) butter
1	7-ounce bag flaked coconut
½	cup chopped pecans
1	8-ounce package cream cheese, softened
1	14-ounce can sweetened condensed milk
1	16-ounce container nondairy whipped topping
2	9-inch deep dish pie crusts, baked
12	ounces caramel topping for ice cream

In a skillet melt the butter and add the coconut and the pecans. Brown until all are golden. Set aside. Blend the cream cheese and the sweetened condensed milk together. Beat until smooth. Fold in the whipped topping. Pour one-fourth of the cream cheese mixture into each pie crust. Drizzle one-fourth of the caramel topping. Add one-fourth of the coconut mixture. Repeat in layers. Freeze. Remove 10 to 15 minutes before serving.

Serves 8.

Susan Wood
Montgomery, Alabama

★ YOGA IS AS YOGA DOES YOGURT PIE ★

1 **8-ounce container yogurt (better with the fruit on the bottom)**

1 **8-ounce container nondairy whipped topping**

1 **graham cracker crust**

In a large bowl mix the yogurt and the whipped topping together. Pour into the pie crust. Chill.

You can put fresh fruit on the top to dress it up, if you like.

Serves 8.

Donna Moore
Knightdale, North Carolina

Elvis in his motorcycle cap and his mom, GLadys, discuss the events to occur later that day in their kitchen at 1034 Audubon Drive, Memphis, Tennessee, July 4, 1956.

★ GOOD OLD-FASHIONED FRIED APPLE PIE ★

1   **8-ounce package dried apple bits**
1   **12-ounce can refrigerator biscuits**

Cook the dried apples according to the directions on the package. Let cool. Roll the canned biscuits extremely thin. Use a small saucer to cut the dough. Place a small amount of the cooled apples on 1 half of each circle. Fold over and crimp the edges together. Punch holes in the pie to let steam escape. Fry in oil over medium heat until both sides done.

Serves 6.

Rosa Nell Powell
The Speer Family

Elvis poses for a cousin in the rec room of his home at 1034 Audubon Drive, Memphis, Tennessee. The relatives had gathered at the Presley home for the Fourth of July and to attend his benefit concert at Russwood Stadium that night. Left to right: Elvis; Billy Smith, Elvis's cousin; Travis Smith, Gladys's brother and Billy's father; Vernon (shaving in the background); on the couch, Gladys and Minnie Mae, Vernon's mother, July 4, 1956.

★ No Fair Peekin' Pecan Dreams ★

1	cup (2 sticks) butter
4	tablespoons confectioners' sugar
2	teaspoons vanilla extract
2	cups sifted all-purpose flour
1	tablespoon water
2	cups broken pecans

Preheat the oven to 300°. In a large bowl cream the butter. Add the sugar and vanilla and blend. Add the flour and water, and blend well. Add the pecans. Put the dough in the refrigerator for 1 hour.

Pinch off small pieces of dough, roll in your palm, and shape into crescents. Place on an ungreased cookie sheet and bake until set but not brown. Roll in sugar when cool.

Makes 2 dozen.

Sue Hacker Hardesty
Cousin of Elvis Presley

EVEN AFTER HIS DEATH, ELVIS'S PRESENCE WAS STILL VERY STRONG AT GRACELAND. ONCE DONNA'S SISTER SUSIE FELT A TUG ON HER ARM WHILE SHE WAS IN THE TV ROOM. SHE TURNED AROUND, THINKING IT WAS ONE OF THE GUARDS, BUT NO ONE WAS THERE. SUSIE THEN WENT INTO THE POOL ROOM AND THE SAME THING HAPPENED. ANOTHER TIME, SUSIE HEARD FOOTSTEPS OVERHEAD WHEN SHE WAS WALKING DIRECTLY BELOW ELVIS'S BEDROOM. SHE THOUGHT IT WAS A MEMBER OF THE STAFF, BUT WHEN SHE WENT UPSTAIRS, NO ONE WAS THERE.

★ ANSWERED PRAYERS PECAN PRALINES ★

4   **cups sugar**

1   **cup water**

1   **cup white corn syrup**

1   **12-ounce can sweetened condensed milk**

2   **teaspoons of vanilla extract**

¼   **cup (½ stick) butter**

2   **cups of pecan pieces**

In a saucepan combine the sugar, water, corn syrup, and sweetened condensed milk. Cook on low heat until all is melted. Heat to a firm ball stage on a candy thermometer. Remove from the heat and add the vanilla, butter, and pecans. Stir until all is firm. Drop onto waxed paper to cool.

Serves 8 to 10.

Pat Early
Donna Presley Early's mother-in-law

Elvis's gravesite in the Meditation Garden at Graceland.

Courtesy of David McGough

★ PLEASE DON'T STOP LOVING ME PECAN PIE ★

1	cup sugar
2	tablespoons sifted all-purpose flour
2	eggs, slightly beaten
1	tablespoon butter
¾	cup light corn syrup
¼	cup cream or milk
1	cup broken pecans
1	teaspoon vanilla extract
1	9-inch unbaked pie crust

Preheat the oven to 350°. In a large bowl mix the sugar and the flour. Add the eggs and butter, and beat. Add the corn syrup and cream and mix well. Stir in the pecans and add the vanilla. Pour into the unbaked pie crust and bake until set.

Serves 6 to 8.

Mim and James Blackwood
The Blackwood Brothers

One of my memories of Elvis is one Christmas Eve. Billy Blackwood and I were in the vicinity of Graceland, and I said, "Why don't we stop in and see if Elvis is here?" Charlie Hodge greeted us and showed us to the living room and said Elvis would be down soon. He came down shortly, and we had a good visit. Then he went upstairs and brought down Lisa Marie for us to see. She was just a baby at the time.

—James Blackwood

★ MARIAN'S PECAN PIE ★

1	cup sugar
1	cup dark Karo syrup
3	eggs, well beaten
2	tablespoons butter, melted (do not substitute margarine)
1	teaspoon vanilla extract
1½	cups whole pecan halves
1	unbaked 9-inch pie shell

A favorite of Elvis Presley's.

Preheat the oven to 375°. In a bowl mix the sugar, corn syrup, eggs, butter, and vanilla. Stir in the pecan halves. Pour the mixture into the pie shell and bake for 15 minutes. Reduce the heat to 350° and bake for another 30 to 40 minutes, or until the pie is set.

Serves 6 to 8.

Marian Cocke
Personal nurse for Elvis Presley

★ Heartbreak Lemon Tart ★

1 **12-ounce can sweetened condensed milk**
½ **cup lemon juice**
1 **8-ounce container nondairy whipped topping**
2 **9-inch frozen pie crusts**

Mix the milk and the lemon juice together. Fill the pie crusts with the mixture. Top with the whipped topping. Chill.
Serves 8.

Edie Hand
Cousin of Elvis Presley

Elvis with cousins Susie, left, and Donna in the back yard of Graceland.

★ LINC'S TARTS ★

1   cup (2 sticks) butter or margarine,
     softened
1   cup sugar
1   teaspoon vanilla extract
1   whole egg, plus 1 egg yolk, well
     beaten
2¼   cups sifted all-purpose flour
1   egg white, slightly beaten

Toppings:
     Finely chopped pecans or walnuts
     Cinnamon sugar
     Colored sprinkles

Preheat the oven to 350°. In a mixing bowl cream together the butter and the sugar. Add the vanilla, the whole egg, and the egg yolk, and beat until fluffy. Blend in the flour until it is thoroughly mixed. Chill the dough overnight.

Roll one-fourth of the dough out thin on a lightly floured board. Cut into the desired shapes. Repeat with the remaining dough.

Place on ungreased baking sheets. Brush the tarts with egg whites and sprinkle with the suggested toppings. Bake for 10 to 12 minutes.

My mother (Edie Hand) and I make these for all of the holidays—using everything from hearts to Santa faces.)

Makes 2 dozen.

Linc Hand
Cousin of Elvis Presley

Linc Hand with grandmother Sue Hacker Hardesty in 1981.

★ Rubberneckin' Rhubarb Crunch ★

Crumb Topping:

1	cup sifted all-purpose flour
¾	cup quick-cooking oats
1	cup firmly packed brown sugar
½	cup melted butter
1	teaspoon ground cinnamon

Filling:

4	cups rhubarb, diced
1	cup sugar
2	tablespoons cornstarch
1	cup water
1	teaspoon vanilla extract

Preheat the oven to 350°. In a medium bowl mix the flour, oats, brown sugar, butter, and cinnamon until crumbly. Press half of it into the bottom of a greased 9-inch pan. Cover with the rhubarb. In a small bowl combine the sugar, cornstarch, water, and vanilla. Pour over the rhubarb. Top with the remaining crumbs. Bake for 1 hour. Cut into squares.

Serves 8 to 10.

Shirley Beattie
Presley-Ites Fan Club
Orlando, Florida

ELVIS RECORDED TWO SONGS AT SAM PHILLIPS'S MEMPHIS RECORDING SERVICE DURING THE SUMMER OF 1953. BUT IT WAS THE RECORDING SESSIONS OF JULY 5 AND 6, 1954, THAT ALTERED HIS LIFE AND THE MUSIC WORLD AS HE LAID THE TRACKS FOR THREE TUNES. WITH SCOTTY MOORE ON GUITAR AND BILL BLACK ON BASS, ELVIS (ALSO ON GUITAR) RECORDED "HARBOR LIGHTS," "THAT'S ALL RIGHT, MAMA," AND "I LOVE YOU BECAUSE."

★ ARE YOU SINCERE PEACH-APRICOT COBBLER ★

½   **cup sugar**

2   **tablespoons cornstarch**

1   **29-ounce can peaches, drained and juice reserved**

1   **11-ounce can apricot halves, drained and juice reserved**

1   **tablespoon butter**

1   **teaspoon ground cinnamon**

1   **teaspoon ground nutmeg**

Topping:

½   **cup all-purpose flour**

½   **cup sugar**

¾   **teaspoon baking powder**

¼   **teaspoon salt**

2   **tablespoons butter, softened**

1   **large egg**

Garnish:

1   **cup heavy cream**

2   **tablespoons honey**

½   **teaspoon ground cinnamon**

Preheat the oven to 400°. In a saucepan mix together the sugar and cornstarch. Stir in ½ cup each of the reserved peach and apricot juices. Cook over medium heat for about 2 minutes, stirring constantly, until the mixture boils and thickens. Remove from the heat. Stir in the butter, cinnamon, and nutmeg. Add the peaches and apricots. Transfer the mixture to a 1½-quart casserole dish.

In a small bowl mix together the flour, sugar, baking powder, salt, butter, and egg. Spoon over the fruit mixture. Bake the cobbler about 30 minutes until the topping is lightly golden Cool slightly on a wire rack.

In a large bowl whip together the cream, honey, and cinnamon, and garnish the warm cobbler just before serving.

Serves 8.

Stella Walton
Alabaster, Alabama

Nash Presley Pritchett visits with fan Stella Walton in the dining room at Graceland.

★ BEACH SHACK PEACH COBBLER ★

½ cup (1 stick) margarine
1 cup sifted self-rising flour
1 cup sugar
1 cup milk
1 28-ounce can peaches
   Whipped topping

Preheat the oven to 350°. In a 9 x13-inch baking dish melt the margarine. In a medium bowl combine the flour, sugar, milk, and peaches. Pour into the melted margarine. Bake until brown. Let cool. Slice and top with a dollop of whipped topping.
     Serves 4 to 6.

Donna Mills
Montgomery, Alabama

★ LEMON STUFF ★

Crust:
2 cups sifted all-purpose flour
1 cup (2 sticks) butter, melted
1 cup chopped nuts

First Layer:
1 8-ounce package cream cheese
1 16-ounce box confectioners' sugar, sifted
1 12-ounce container nondairy whipped topping

Second Layer:
2 10-ounce cans lemon pie filling

Top Layer:
1 cup nondairy whipped topping
1 cup chopped nuts

Preheat the oven to 325°. In a medium bowl combine the flour, butter, and nuts. Press into a 9 x 13-inch pan. Bake for 15 minutes. Let cool.
     In a large bowl mix together the cream cheese, confectioners' sugar, and whipped topping. Spread over the crust.
     Spread the lemon pie filling over the cream cheese layer.
     Cover the lemon layer with the whipped topping and sprinkle with the chopped nuts.
     Serves 6.

Faye Spivey
Montgomery, Alabama

★ CHOCOLATE GRAHAM CRUSH ★

20   graham crackers, crushed
1   12-ounce can sweetened condensed
     milk
1   12-ounce package chocolate chips

Preheat the oven to 350°. In a large bowl mix the ingredients together. Spoon into a 9-inch square baking dish. Bake for 25 minutes.
Serves 8 to 10.

Shirley Beattie
Presley-Ites Fan Club
Orlando, Florida

★ CHOCOLATE WAFER DELIGHTS ★

     Nondairy whipped topping
1   15-ounce box chocolate wafer cook-
     ies
1   cup chopped nuts or cherries

Spoon a small amount of the whipped topping on each wafer cookie. Top with chopped nuts or cherries. Place them in a container and let them sit in the refrigerator overnight or slightly longer until the wafers have been softened by the topping.
The number of servings depends on how many you make!

Christy Rogers
Dora, Alabama

★ Sweet Elvis ★

1   quart applesauce
2   eggs
1   glass sweet red wine
1   tablespoon sugar
2   sweet pears, cut up
1   large banana, sliced
2   cups fresh (or canned, drained)
      pineapple chunks
     Whipped cream

In a large nonmetallic mixing bowl combine the first 4 ingredients and mix with an electric mixer for 2 minutes. Stir in the pears, banana, and pineapple. Place in the refrigerator for at least 1 hour. Spoon into bowls, top with whipped cream, and serve.
     Serves 4.

Andolyn Lensen
Beverwyk, Holland

ELVIS WAS VERY GENEROUS WITH HIS MONEY. HE DONATED MILLIONS OVER THE YEARS TO CHARITY, BUT DIDN'T LIKE TO RAISE ATTENTION TO IT. HE HELD A BENEFIT CONCERT FOR MEMPHIS CHARITIES EARLY IN HIS CAREER, WHICH RAISED $50,000. AFTER THAT, HE WAS UNABLE TO SCHEDULE CONCERTS EVERY YEAR, SO HE WOULD JUST SEND A $50,000 CHECK TO MAKE UP FOR IT. IN ADDITION HE WOULD MAKE PERSONAL GESTURES FOR PEOPLE. ONE CHILD IN MEMPHIS WAS DYING OF CANCER AND SAID HE WANTED A LETTER FROM ELVIS BEFORE HE DIED. ELVIS VISITED THE CHILD, AND, EVEN AFTER THE FAMILY MOVED AWAY, ELVIS CONTINUED TO WRITE THE LITTLE BOY.

★ CHERRY-BERRY BINGE ★

1	cup (1 stick) butter or margarine, melted
2	cups sifted all-purpose flour
1	cup chopped pecans
1	16-ounce box confectioners' sugar
1	8-ounce package cream cheese
1	12-ounce container nondairy whipped topping
1	10-ounce can cherry pie filling

Preheat the oven to 350°. In a large bowl mix the melted butter, flour, and pecans. Press into a thin layer that covers the bottom of an 8 x12-inch baking dish. Bake for 30 minutes or until it is brown. Cool the crust.

In a large bowl mix the confectioners' sugar, cream cheese, and whipped topping, and spread over the cooled crust. Spread the cherry pie filing over the top. Refrigerate.

Serves 6.

Kim Blackburn Poss
Cousin of Elvis Presley

★ CHERRY HILL DELIGHT ★

1	15-ounce can cherry pie filling
1	10-ounce can crushed pineapple
1	18-ounce box yellow cake mix (unmixed)
¾	cup (1½ sticks) margarine, melted
1½	cups chopped nuts

Preheat the oven to 350°. Layer the ingredients in a greased 9 x 13-inch baking dish in the order given. Bake for 45 minutes.

Serves 6.

Judy Hill Sargent
Birmingham, Alabama

★ ECHOES OF LOVE EGG CUSTARD ★

2½ cups milk, scalded
½ cup sugar
1 teaspoon vanilla extract
4 eggs, beaten
1 9-inch pie crust

Preheat the oven to 400°. In a large bowl combine the milk, sugar, vanilla, and eggs, and mix together well. Place in the pie crust. Bake for 20 to 25 minutes or until a knife inserted in the center comes out clean.

Serves 6 to 8.

Etta Slater
Rogersville, Tennessee

Elvis takes a break with girlfriend Linda Thompson during a karate demonstration.

★ MAMA'S BANANA PUDDING ★

1   8-ounce container nondairy
      whipped topping
2   cups sweet milk
1   12-ounce can sweetened condensed
      milk
1   3-ounce box instant vanilla pudding
1   8-ounce box vanilla wafers
4   bananas

I have fond memories of my mom making this dish for the family while I was growing up. It was always one of my favorites.—Edie Hand

In a large bowl combine the whipped topping and the sweet milk. Add the sweetened condensed milk, and mix well. Add the dry pudding mix and beat well. In a separate bowl place a layer of vanilla wafers and a layer of bananas. Pour the pudding over it, and put in the refrigerator to chill.
Serves 4 to 6.

*Sue Hacker Hardesty
Cousin of Elvis Presley*

★ BIG BOSS MAN BANANA PUDDING ★

1   cup sugar
¼   cup cornstarch
3   egg yolks, well beaten
3   cups whole milk
3   tablespoons butter (do not substi-
       tute margarine)
1   teaspoon vanilla extract
      Banana slices
1   box vanilla wafers
      Whipped cream

In a saucepan over medium heat , cook the first 4 ingredients, stirring constantly until the pudding thickens. Remove from the heat and stir in the butter and vanilla. Allow the custard to cool. Line the bottom of a glass or ceramic bowl with banana slices and vanilla wafers. Pour half of the custard on top. Add another layer of bananas and wafers and then the remainder of the custard. Cover with plastic wrap and refrigerate until cold. Top with whipped cream.

Note: You could use the egg whites to do a meringue for the pudding, but to me it always toughens the bananas to put them in the oven, so I opt for the whipped cream!

*Marian Cocke
Personal Nurse for Elvis Presley*

★ BOSSA NOVA BABY BUTTERMILK SALAD ★

1   **20-ounce can crushed pineapple**
1   **6-ounce box strawberry gelatin**
2   **cups buttermilk**
1   **9-ounce container nondairy**
       whipped topping
½   **cup nuts**

In a saucepan heat the pineapple with juice. Add the gelatin mix and stir until it is dissolved. Set aside to cool until it is almost cold. Add the buttermilk, whipped topping, and nuts. Mix well. Pour into a 9 x13-inch baking dish and refrigerate.

    Serves 6.

Jean Arrington
Union Springs, Alabama

Elvis visits with a friend.

★ CHARRO CHERRY SALAD ★

1   12-ounce can sweetened condensed
     milk
1   8-ounce carton sour cream
1   12-ounce container nondairy
     whipped topping
1   20-ounce can crushed pineapple,
     well drained
1   tablespoon lemon juice
1   cup chopped nuts
1   15-ounce can cherry pie filling

In a large bowl mix all of the ingredients together, placing the cherry pie filling in last. Place in a 9 x13-inch baking dish and refrigerate for several hours before serving. Salad can be frozen and cut into squares. **Serves 6.**

Jean Arrington
Union Springs, Alabama

From Elvis Flick to Television (Part five)

Match the actress who worked with Elvis to the TV series they starred or co-starred in.

SITCOM U.S. FEMALES

1. Joan Blondell *(Stay Away Joe)*
2. Donna Douglas *(Frankie & Johnny)*
3. Barbara Eden *(Flaming Star)*
4. Shelley Fabares *(Girl Happy)*
5. Anissa Jones *(The Trouble With Girls)*
6. Carolyn Jones *(King Creole)*
7. Hope Lange *(Wild in the Country)*
8. Mary Tyler Moore *(Change of Habit)*
9. Pat Priest *(Easy Come, Easy Go)*
10. Deborah Walley *(Spinout)*

A. *The Addams Family*
B. *The Beverly Hillbillies*
C. *Coach*
D. *Family Affair*
E. *The Ghost and Mrs. Muir*
F. *Here Come the Brides*
G. *I Dream of Jeannie*
H. *Mary Tyler Moore Show*
I. *The Mothers-In-Law*
J. *The Munsters*

ANSWERS: 1. F, 2. B, 3. G, 4. C, 5. D, 6. A, 7. E, 8. H, 9. I, 10. I

★ PRETZEL SALAD ANNIE ★

2   cups thin stick pretzels, broken into
       pieces
¾   cup (1½ sticks) butter
2   teaspoons sugar

First Topping:
1   8-ounce package cream cheese
1   cup sugar
1   8-ounce container nondairy
       whipped topping

Second Topping:
2   3-ounce packages strawberry
       gelatin
1   cup boiling water
2   10-ounce packages frozen strawber-
       ries (or fresh, if in season)

Preheat the oven to 400°. In a medium bowl combine the pretzels, butter, and sugar, and press into a baking dish. Bake for 8 minutes. Let cool.

In a medium bowl mix together the cream cheese, sugar, and whipped topping and spread over the crust. In a large bowl mix the gelatin and the water. Let cool. Add the strawberries. Pour on top of the cream cheese mixture. When it begins to thicken, refrigerate.

Serves 4.

Kim Blackburn Poss
Cousin of Elvis Presley

Elvis with friends.

★ CADILLAC CARAMEL APPLE SALAD ★

6   to 8 apples, cored and cut into
       chunks
4   or 5 chilled chocolate-coated
       caramel bars, cut into bite-sized
       pieces
1   8-ounce container nondairy
       whipped topping, slightly thawed

In a large bowl stir together the apples and caramel bars. (I like to do this in a pretty glass bowl.) Fold in the thawed whipped topping and refrigerate.

This is guaranteed to please at Christmas time. I use red and green apples for a festive look.

Serves 6.

Kris Grover
Corona, Georgia

★ MINNIE'S ORIGINAL DESSERT ★

2   3-ounce boxes cherry gelatin
4   large bananas, sliced
1   cup chopped pecans
2   cups miniature marshmallows

Prepare the gelatin according to the instructions on the box. Add the sliced bananas to the gelatin, and then add the chopped pecans and the marshmallows. Stir and refrigerate until the gelatin is set.

Serves 4.

Minnie Lou Mills
Union Springs, Alabama

★ PISTACHIO SALAD ★

1   **20-ounce can crushed pineapple**

1   **3-ounce box pistachio instant pudding mix**

1½ **cups miniature marshmallows**

1   **cup chopped nuts (optional)**

1   **8-ounce container nondairy whipped topping**

In a large bowl combine the crushed pineapple with the juice and instant pudding. Mix together. Add the marshmallows and the nuts. Stir until well blended. Fold in the whipped topping. Pour into a serving dish and refrigerate until you are ready to serve.

    Serves 6.

Carol Rogers
Dora, Alabama

Elvis lights up the stage!

Courtesy of Hazel Johnson

★ BLACK AND WHITE SUNDAE ★

2	scoops of vanilla ice cream
	Hot chocolate fudge sauce
	Real whipped cream
	Crushed walnuts
	A cherry

Hundreds of fans of the Nancy comic strip participated in an ice cream sundae contest in June 1997. This recipe by Molly Erlich, age 80, of Manchester, New Hampshire, was a winner.

It's 2 scoops of vanilla ice cream, smothered in hot chocolate fudge sauce and real whipped cream and topped with crushed walnuts and a cherry.

A Sundae fit for the King

Nancy, star of the classic comic strip, has had a love affair with ice cream ever since cartoonist Ernie Bushmiller created Nancy and Sluggo in the 1930s. The strip is carried in hundreds of newspapers today and is drawn in the classic style by brothers Guy and Brad Gilchrist, rock 'n' roll fans who have introduced Nancy and her Aunt Fritzi to the charms of Elvis.

True classics, Elvis's timeless tunes on vinyl 45s and Nancy's quirky comic strip antics will never go out of style. Nancy's contribution to this cookbook reflects the tender tastes of an earlier time—a simple black and white sundae.

★ CHART-TOPPER DESSERT FROSTING ★

1   **3-ounce box flavored instant pudding (your choice of flavor)**
¼   **cup confectioners' sugar**
¾   **cup milk**
1   **8-ounce container nondairy whipped topping**

In a large bowl mix the dry pudding, sugar, and milk together. Then fold in the whipped topping. Whip and chill.
Makes enough to cover a dessert.

Heidi Rutharat
Glendale, Arizona

Elvis's Top Twenty Hits That Were Not No. 1

I Was the One, #19
Blue Suede Shoes, #20
Any Way You Want Me (That's How I Will Be), #20
Love Me, #2
When My Blue Moon Turns to Gold Again, #19
Loving You, #20
Treat Me Nice, #18
I Beg of You, #8
Wear My Ring Around Your Neck, #2
Doncha' Think It's Time, #15
One Night, #4
I Got Stung, #8
Now and Then There's Such a Fool as I, #2
I Need Your Love Tonight, #4
My Wish Came True, #12
Fame and Fortune, #17
I Gotta Know, #20
Flaming Star, #14
I Feel So Bad, #5
Little Sister, #5
Marie's the Name of His Latest Flame, #4
Can't Help Falling in Love, #2
Follow That Dream, #15
She's Not You, #5
Return to Sender/Where Do You Come From, #2

One Broken Heart for Sale, #11
You're the Devil in Disguise, #3
Bossa Nova Baby, #8
Kissin' Cousins, #12
Such a Night, #16
Ask Me, #12
Ain't That Loving You Baby, #16
Crying in the Chapel, #3
Such an Easy Question, #11
I'm Yours, #11
Puppet on a String, #14
Love Letters, #19
If I Can Dream, #12
In the Ghetto, #3
Don't Cry Daddy, #6
Kentucky Rain, #16
The Wonder of You/Mama Like the Roses, #9
You Don't Have to Say You Love Me/Patch It Up, #11
Burning Love, #2
Separate Ways, #20
Steamroller Blues, #17
If You Talk in Your Sleep, #17
Promised Land/It's Midnight, #14
My Boy, #20
Way Down, #18

Index

★ ★

★ D ★

★ R ★

Printed in the USA
CPSIA information can be obtained
at www.ICGtesting.com
JSHW052015140824
68134JS00027B/2480